Jamestown Rediscovery III

William M. Kelso
Nicholas M. Luccketti
Beverly A. Straube

The Association for the Preservation
of Virginia Antiquities
1997

Dedication

To Peter Dun Grover, Executive Director of the APVA, who generously released the long coveted keys to the city.

Graphics by Jamie E. May
Design and production by Elliott Jordan

Printed in The United States of America

ISBN: 0-917565-05-3

Preface

The following pages describe and illustrate the major discoveries of the *APVA Jamestown Rediscovery* archaeological project's third season, 1996. Research is a never-ending pursuit and therefore new information appears in this volume about discoveries from 1994-95 as well. Historical archaeology must be a dual process: archaeology *and* history. So, following a summary of the most recent archaeological discoveries, Chapter II, by Nicholas Luccketti, reviews what documents tell us about the military and colonial experiences the early settlers brought to Jamestown and how they may have influenced its creation. Chapter III, by Beverly Straube, combines artifact descriptions and documentary evidence to bring meaning to significant artifacts. While computer technology makes it possible to publish so soon after a field excavation season, the lack of analysis time renders this publication necessarily incomplete and its conclusions tentative. Nonetheless, the extremely significant 1996 results convincingly relate to the discovery of the first Jamestown settlement and call for rapid publication. Volume III is the third of an anticipated series that will be published annually, including Volume XIV in 2007, the 400th anniversary of Jamestown's founding—and beyond.

Acknowledgements

Archaeology is usually a team effort and the name of this project, *APVA Jamestown Rediscovery*, reflects that. It draws on the discoveries of a century of Jamestown archaeologists, hence "rediscovery" of their work. The list of those who helped in the past and in 1996 alone is so long that I will unwittingly leave someone out of the credits that follow. For that unavoidable mistake, I apologize in advance but try to include everyone.

Without the vision for preserving Jamestown by the Association for the Preservation of Virginia Antiquities (APVA), the site which we now know holds treasures of early Jamestown would have long been reclaimed by the James River. I offer my most enduring gratitude to Mary Jeffery Galt, Annie Galt, and Samuel Yonge for their efforts to save Jamestown a century ago. For keeping the dream of unlocking the long-held secrets of APVA Jamestown alive and for being so essential in making that dream a reality, I express my deepest gratitude to the late Mary Douthat Higgins. I am most grateful to APVA Executive Director Peter Dun Grover, to whom these pages are dedicated, for his enthusiastic support and for continuing to wholeheartedly embrace an archaeological vision for the APVA. I also express my appreciation to Warren Billings, Chairman of the *APVA Jamestown Rediscovery* Archaeological Board, and to its members. I thank, as well, the members of the APVA Executive Board and President Robert Giles for their confidence in the program during these early years. I also thank the Governor of Virginia, George Allen, for his support and announcement of the discovery of the fort and the Virginia General Assembly for their support, especially Senator Thomas Norment. The National Endowment for the Humanities, the National Geographic Society, the Jessie Ball duPont Fund, the National Society Colonial Daughters of the Seventeenth Century, and the National Society Daughters of Founders and Patriots of America have all contributed to the success of the project as well.

The *Jamestown Rediscovery* team is a rare group of steadfastly dedicated people who individually and collectively bring multiple talents to the project. For their essential contributions I wish to express my sincere gratitude to senior research archaeologist, Nicholas Luccketti, for his skillful field and documentary research and for writing Chapter II; to curator, Beverly Straube, for her extraordinary artifact research and for writing Chapter III; to conservator, Elliott Jordan, for what seems his limitless talents and especially for publishing brochures and this booklet; to staff archaeologist, Eric Deetz, for his remarkable field, educational, and archival skills; to Jamie May, for her insightful excavation, recording, and remarkable computer graphic design work in this booklet; and to Michael Lavin, for his fine conservation work. For their trowels and experience, thanks to Eric Klingelhofer, Alain Outlaw, Carter Hudgins, Phil Levy, and John Coombs. Sincere thanks to Douglas Owsley, David Hunt, and the Smithsonian Institution for their forensic analysis. Special appreciation to Michael Westfall for his generous donations of equipment and for his diligent volunteer excavation skills. Thanks to the field excavation efforts of Douglas Rixey, Joanne Robbins, and Chris Slappy and our Summer Institute teachers, especially Camille Hedrick and her hearty Gloucester High School students, Thad Pardue for his usual Herculean excavation effort, and David Hepburn and Macon Parker for their field contributions.

I respectfully thank the APVA staff: Louis Malon, who kept the books; Elizabeth Kostelny, who assisted in grant writing; and Ann Berry, who created and managed our exceptional volunteer interpreters program. A special thanks to the volunteers, without whom we could barely manage to get anything done on site. Also, thanks to Bob Berry for his assistance with exhibit graphics and especially for our essential ability to do NASA X-rays as part of the conservation program. My appreciation to the volunteer efforts of The College of William and Mary geologist emeritus, Jerre Johnson, and geologist Glen Izett. The project was facilitated by Alec Gould, Superintendent of the Colonial National Historical Park. I am most grateful to him and his staff: Jim Haskett, Jane Sundberg, Diane Stallings, Curt Gaul, David Riggs, and especially to Bill Warder, one of our most enthusiastic interpreters and "mud daubers."

Much gratitude to Tim Kolly who made the "fort announcement" such a special event in archaeological history; to Mark St. John Erickson for his insightful reporting; and to Mary Ellen Stumpf for getting APVA development seriously rolling. Special thanks to Julie Grover and Ellen Kelso for proofreading, and to Ellen for steadfastly "managing" the Yeardley House Inn and always being there to listen.

WMK, Jamestown, VA, 4/16/97

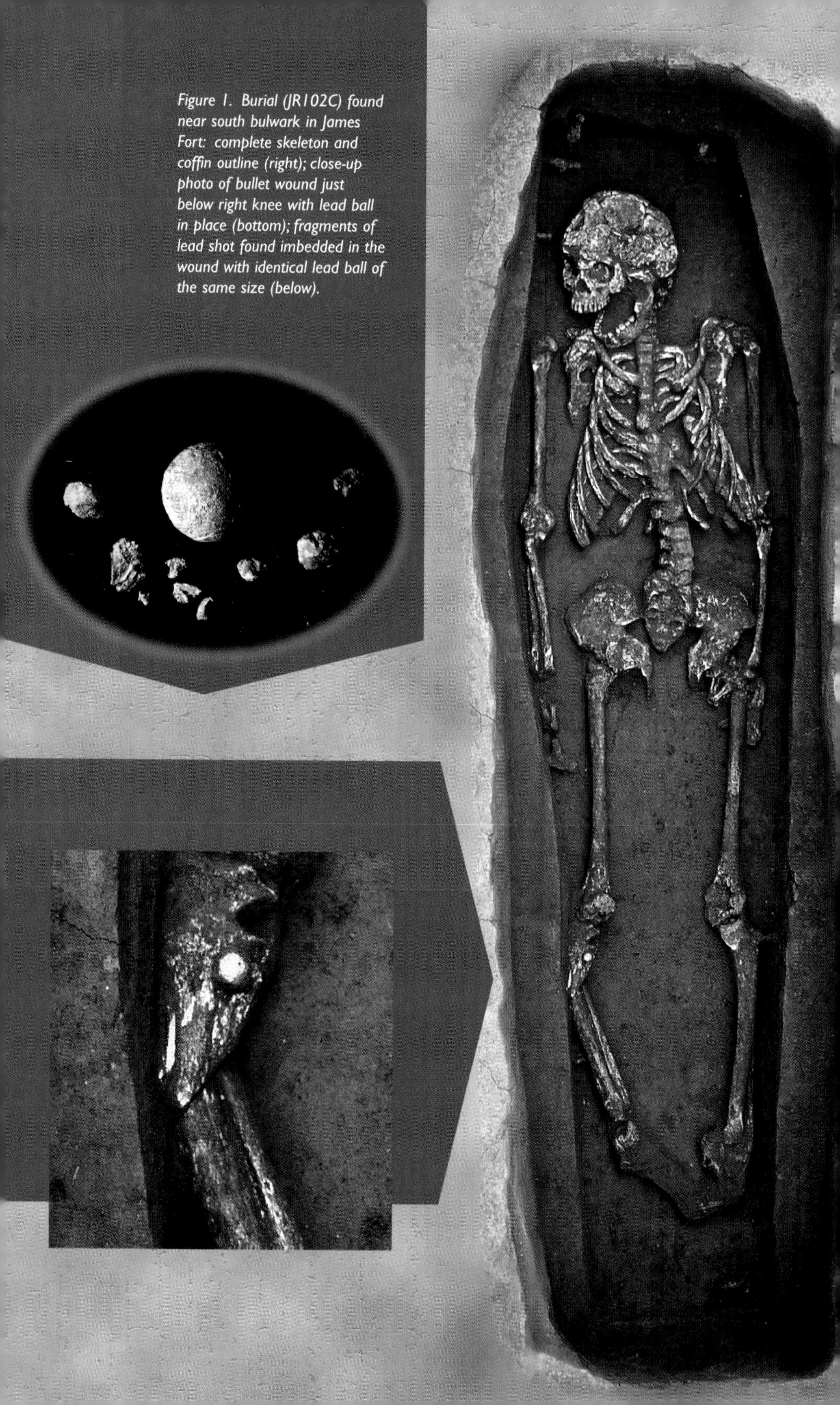

Figure 1. Burial (JR102C) found near south bulwark in James Fort: complete skeleton and coffin outline (right); close-up photo of bullet wound just below right knee with lead ball in place (bottom); fragments of lead shot found imbedded in the wound with identical lead ball of the same size (below).

Introduction

JR102C

Death never ceases to remind me how little I understand life. That was especially true when I came face to face with the burial of a young man in the remnants of the newly discovered 1607 James Fort at Jamestown, Virginia. Nearly 400 years have passed since his death, so it will be next to impossible to know much about his life. Nevertheless, meeting those remains helped me more clearly know just how difficult it was for the New World adventurers to begin the spread of English-style civilization to the ends of the earth.

This 5'5", 19-year-old white man apparently died from a gunshot wound in the leg and was buried inside James Fort. James Fort was a stockaded triangular enclosure built in a few weeks in June 1607 to repel the native Powhatan Indians who had quickly become a serious threat to the colonists. It is unlikely that any native person shot this settler, although it is conceivable that the Powhatans were quick to seek the same firepower as their adversaries.[1] In that case JR102C (our scientific name for the burial) was probably the victim of "friendly fire," accidental or otherwise. We know full well that disease, starvation, bad water, and the intermittent attacks from the Powhatan Indians felled two-thirds of the settlers in the first few months of the settlement. To see hard evidence that death by their own weapons, and perhaps by their own hands, was yet another threat to the colony makes the Jamestown mission seem all the more impossible. It is one thing to find the armor they wore, the guns they shot, and the thousands of things from everyday life they left in the ground, but quite another to find the very bones of those who made the ultimate sacrifice. That is the near time travel experience that archaeology can sometimes provide and did at the APVA Jamestown Rediscovery Project in 1996. Somehow, in a much more intimate way, we now know more vividly about the struggle to found English America.

While we may never know for sure who is or who shot JR102C, there is a slight hope of identification. We can conclude that he was killed early in the settlement of Jamestown by the fact that fragmented artifacts accidentally mixed in with the dirt covering the coffin either were objects used by pre-Jamestown Indians on the site or were objects dating to the first settlement years. Also, the fact that he rated a coffin may indicate he was among the

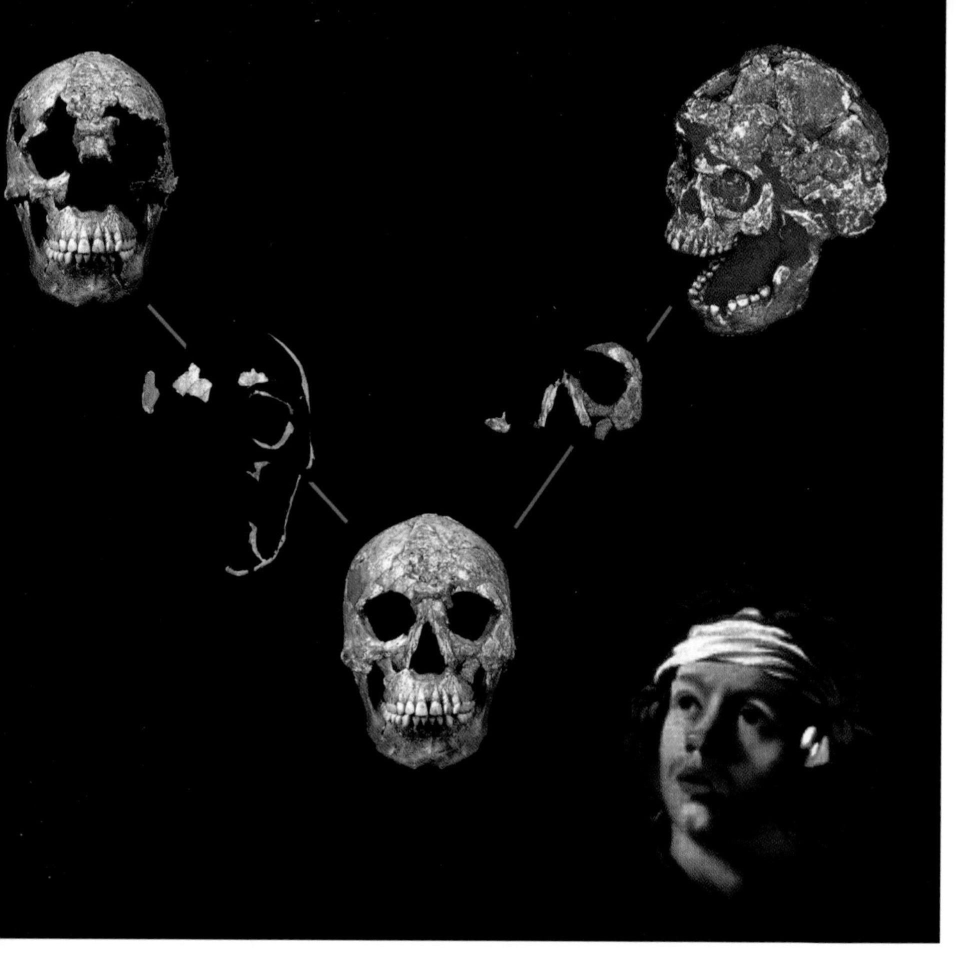

Figure 2. Digital reconstruction of skull from burial JR102C combining fragments taken from the photo of the crushed skull in place (upper right); photo of mended skull (upper left); fragments taken from both the crushed and mended skull (middle left and right); reconstructed skull (center); and face of young soldier from a 1650s painting.

"gentlemen" of the colony. Captain John Smith wrote of the death of eight gentlemen among the first 104 colonists, and George Percy lists 12 gentlemen's deaths before his own weakened condition apparently ended his reporting (September 1607).[2] Of course, news of a death by "friendly fire" would hardly be anything to write home about, especially when much needed supplies and potential colonists waited in the wings for the next ship to America. But given that JR102C was shot and buried in those early months when people were healthy enough to still make coffins for gentlemen, then JR102C could well be any one of these earliest recorded deaths. William Bruster (Brewster) died August 8, 1607 "from a wound given by the savages" (gunshot?) and Jerome Alikock died from a "wound" six days later. Other gentlemen dying early but of unnamed causes include: Thomas Gower 8/16/1607, John Martine 8/19/1607, Drue Piggase 8/19/1607, Kellam Throgmorton 8/28/1607, and Thomas Studley 8/28/1607.[3]

Records indicate that only one gentleman was shot. Captain George Kendall was arrested in September 1607 and was seemingly charged with treason. It is unclear whether or not this accusation by then President Ratcliffe was true. At first Kendall was imprisoned on one of the ships and later released without his weapons. Then, after a trial, he was "shot."[4] While he cannot be completely ruled out as the identity of JR102C, a leg wound certainly is a cruel and unusual way to execute someone. But that leg wound may have been only part of his trauma. A more immediately fatal shot could have passed completely through his body, never leaving any marks on the surviving bones. Kendall, however, may have been in his forties when he came to Virginia, while JR102C died at around age 19. Perhaps the reconstruction of the face on the skull might produce a clue to his identity. In the meantime, JR102C remains Anglo-America's oldest unknown soldier and perhaps her oldest unsolved murder.

Who JR102C was and why he died are intriguing questions. But perhaps more importantly our colonist is one face in a crowd that is otherwise difficult to know. We seem to have most of their names, but a name is not a face, a personality, nor a biography. There are only two known likenesses of any of the original adventurers: Captain John Smith and George Percy. We do have biog-

Figure 3. Engraving of Captain John Smith (left) and George Percy (right), the only two likenesses known of any of the 104 original Jamestown settlers.

raphies of some of the other more prominent "gentlemen." They ranged in age from 27 to 47 and, significantly, before coming to Jamestown, many served for a number of years in the military service of the United Provinces of the Netherlands in their long war against Spain.[5] That they came to Virginia to seek fame and fortune there can be no doubt. That, like JR102C, the experience was something less than they had hoped is tragic. It is equally tragic that these gentlemen adventurers must have felt the sting of failure as the reality of Virginia sank in and yet could never know that eventually all American political, judicial, and largely cultural identity springs from their own first efforts in Virginia. While we must never forget the disastrous effect their coming had on the native population, the ultimate result of the English colony at Jamestown on the course of world history demands that the archaeological remains of these first "discoverers" be treated with deep respect.

Trail to James Fort

How did we come to find JR102C and his fort? It was not easy and it did not happen overnight. In fact, for me it all began over three decades ago during a typical dull March day in an Ohio college library. Tired of memorizing names and dates for a history exam, I decided to cheer up by reading about Virginia, where I heard the sun always shines and American history, my second passion in life, was a very serious subject. Somewhere among the literature, an aerial photo of Jamestown Island spread out before me. I was totally mesmerized. The focus of the picture was the archaeological excavations in 1957 that were making a major effort to learn about the buried town for the 350th celebration of its founding. The photo was my first view of Jamestown—its lush unspoiled woodland, manicured village lawn, and the spacious James River shore. But the strict order of a gridiron of archaeological trenches crisscrossing the grassy park overwhelmed the view. I never once thought that archaeology could ever happen so close to my own time and place in history. At that time practically all my knowledge of archaeology had come from those vivid National Geographic photo essays on the pyramids. Never much of a spectator, I could not help imagining digging in that "ancient" Jamestown soil with my own hands. I was fascinated with the accompanying story of the 350-year-old first settlement, but at the same time sad to learn that Jamestown was all found and dug up, or so it seemed. So much for that. Nonetheless, I now know that at that time I subconsciously vowed to someday go to Jamestown, if for no other reason than to see the already exhumed remains for myself.

Figure 4. A 1955 aerial view of the excavations of the eastern part of Jamestown conducted by the National Park Service showing grid of search trenches primarily used to explore the vast acreage and to determine the location of buildings.

Eventually I let my interest in early American history lead me to graduate school at the College of William and Mary in Williamsburg, Virginia. Naturally, my first visit to that area found me walking the ruins at nearby Jamestown Island in search of the 1607 fort that must surely have been uncovered in 1955. There, I was immediately drawn to the James River bank, the Association for the Preservation of Virginia Antiquities' moss-covered reconstructed church, the statues of Pocahontas and Captain John Smith, and a curious glass window in the side of the earthen Civil War fort nearby. The glass protected an archaeologically exposed profile of the dirt in the fort bank. It showed the actual dirt surfaces that made up the bank: (A) the Civil War zone complete with Minié balls on top of (B) the dark band of "colonial" trash sitting on the deepest deposit, and (C) a lighter soil containing "arrowheads" and prehistoric Indian pottery. It was clearly a layer cake in time: pre-1607 at the bottom, the 1607-1776 Colonial period in the middle, and the 1861-65 Civil War era on top. That seemed so simple—what is older is deeper, artifacts tell time, and the earth can be an index of American history. Then I naively asked a park ranger where the old fort site was. I was surprised when he pointed to a lone cypress tree growing way off shore and said, "Unfortunately out there and lost for good." Confused, I looked back at the dirt under glass that said "colonial" and asked

Figure 5. National Park Service archaeologist Joel Shiner next to the cross sectional trench dug into the dirt bank of Jamestown's Civil War earthwork fort showing: (A) Civil War period, (B) Colonial period, (C) Pre-1607 Virginia Indian period (background), and a curious "L-shaped" excavated ditch (right foreground). This excavated cross section was left visible to Jamestown visitors as an archaeological exhibit for several years after the 1955 digging.

again, "but what about here?" He thought for a moment and then replied with a shrug of his shoulders which I took as a "maybe."

A few years and much fieldwork later, I had become an archaeologist specializing in the British Colonial America period and learning, with my colleagues, about the often forgotten American century—the 1600s. Most of our work focused on rescuing farm sites along the James which were being "rediscovered" by real restate developers and "resettled" by retirees. The more we learned from the earth about the 17th century, however, the more we thought of the possibility that the site of the first decade of Jamestown settlement might lie on APVA land yet unexplored. Indeed the "colonial level" under that glass exhibit at the Civil War fort looked better and better, especially when Nicholas Luccketti, Bly Straube, and I restudied the field notes and artifacts from the 1955 National Park Service excavations. Everything looked like the footprints of the relatively insubstantial wooden palisade defense "forts" we had since found elsewhere on the James, and the finds were old and military enough to have been used at James Fort. So when the APVA embarked on a campaign to do something significant with its property on Jamestown Island by the 400th anniversary of Jamestown in 2007, there were a number of archaeologists ready to be called. Their interest focused immediately not 100 feet from the site of the glass cross section. Consequently, nearly 33 years to the day after I first set foot on the island, the Governor of Virginia announced that the remains of 1607 James Fort had been found. Amazingly enough, I did not have to miss out on digging at James Fort after all.

Figure 6. Virginia Governor George Allen inspects the Jamestown settler's grave on September 12, 1996, the day he publicly announced the "rediscovery" of James Fort.

Figure 7. William Shakespeare (right), a signet ring found at Jamestown in 1996 (below), and an artist's rendering of the wreck of the Jamestown supply ship, Sea Venture *in Bermuda in 1609 (bottom). The ring is engraved with the Strachey family heraldic crest (a displayed eagle with a cross on its breast). William Strachey's written account of the* Sea Venture *wreck inspired Shakespeare's famous play,* The Tempest, *and Strachey's description of James Fort in the same manuscript is the most detailed record of early Jamestown.*

Shakespearean Americans

...commending our souls to God, committed the ship to the mercy of the sea.[6] William Strachey

Mariners: All lost! To prayer, to prayers. All lost![7] William Shakespeare

In the late fall of 1996, excavations in the southeastern bulwark of the James Fort site recovered a brass finger ring finely engraved with the figure of a large bird and with what appears to be a cross on its breast. It is a signet ring commonly used for impressing wax seals on documents. Some of these rings bear the official heraldic crest of their owner's family, an official symbol registered at the College of Arms in London. A "displayed" eagle embossed with a cross-crosslet on its breast is the official crest of the Strachey family. William Strachey played a significant role in the Jamestown settlement. Heading for Virginia in 1609, Strachey got as far as Bermuda where the supply ship, the *Sea Venture*, wrecked in a hurricane. The survivors stayed for the next several months building replacement vessels in which they sailed to Jamestown by May 1610. Strachey remained at Jamestown for less than a year, but during that time he became the Secretary of the Colony. He wrote an eloquent letter to an unnamed "dear lady" about his experience in the *Sea Venture* disaster and his time at Jamestown. The letter probably reached England with him in late 1610.[8] There is little doubt that among the English readers of this manuscript was none other than William Shakespeare, for some of the theme, details, and setting for his famous play, *The Tempest*, almost certainly draws directly on Strachey's Bermuda experience. But more than an interesting, indirect Shakespearean cameo appearance for Jamestown history, Strachey's ring comments on the caliber of the men who ventured to Jamestown, and it serves to set the settlement in time. Jamestown was settled at the same time William Shakespeare was at the height of his career. And Shakespeare was dead and gone before the *Mayflower* landed at Plymouth.

Strachey returned to an apparently unhappy life in England. There, in 1621, he died in poverty leaving this rather depressing verse:

Hark! Twas the trump of death that blew
My hour has come. False world adieu
Thy pleasures have betrayed me so
That I to death untimely go.[9]

Strachey may not have been so bitter had he lived to see his Bermuda and Jamestown manuscript published in 1625 or the priceless value his descriptions of Jamestown came to hold today. His "True Reportory" includes one of the few and the most informative descriptions of early Jamestown, particularly James Fort as he saw it in June 1609:

> *"the fort growing since to more perfection, is now at this present in this manner: ...about half an acre...is cast almost into the form of a triangle and so palisaded. The south side next the river (howbeit extended in a line or curtain sixscore foot more in length than the other two, by reason the advantage of the ground doth require) contains 140 yards, the west and east sides a hundred only. At every angle or corner, where the lines meet, a bulwark or watchtower is raised and in each bulwark a piece or two well mounted....And thus enclosed, as I said, round with a palisade of planks and strong posts, four feet deep in the ground, of young oaks, walnuts, etc...the fort is called, in honor of His Majesty's name, Jamestown. The principal gate from the town, through the palisade, opens to the river, as at each bulwark there is a gate likewise to go forth and at every gate a demiculverin and so in the market-place."*[10]

Archaeological discoveries at Jamestown in 1996 proved to be the remnants of what Strachey saw, and there is every reason to believe they are also traces of George Percy's "triangular-wise" 1607 James Fort with three "half moon" bulwarks at the corners[11] and John Smith's 1608 "five-side" Jamestown with "three bulwarks."[12]

WMK

Figure 8. Model of James Fort, based on an interpretation of written descriptions, 1607-1610, and exhibited in the Jamestown Visitors Center since 1957.

Figure 9. Artist Sydney King's hypothetical view of Jamestown as it may have been expanded to the east after the fir of 1608 (John Smith's "five-sided" town?).

Figure 10. View of the Jamestown Rediscovery excavations, September 1996 (above), and the same view with a superimposed digital reconstruction of the Fort (below). Including the south palisade wall (left, background), the south bastion (left, center) with earth bank "rampart" and nearby "dry moat" (center), and the east wall line (right, foreground), as indicated by the archaeological footprint of the original construction.

by William Kelso

Chapter I

Beginning Rediscovery

Removal of the upper foot of plowed soil in the yard south of the church during the course of three digging seasons (1994-1996) uncovered a number of soil disturbances in the deeper clay that prove beyond a reasonable doubt to be the remnants of 1607-1625(?) James Fort. These early 17th-century features are part of the footprints of the defense work, including sections of two fort walls, part of a projecting corner defensive construction known as a bulwark or bastion, one of the James Fort interior timber buildings, three backfilled pits, a series of ditches and postholes and a grave. The plowed soil and the fill in these features held over, 150,000 artifacts, most dating to the first quarter of the 1600s. A surprising number of these objects were over 400 years old, including arms, armor, ammunition, pottery, coins, political tokens and scrap from the manufacture of copper jewelry for the Indian trade and glassmaking.

In 1996 clearing of the plowzone near the river bank seawall toward the churchyard uncovered a narrow trench curving from south to north and a larger and deeper trench that mirrored the smaller trench curve 9' to the north and east (see fig. 11). It is clear from the parallel nature of the narrow and wide trenches that they are parts of the same construction. There is every reason to believe that the narrow curved trench was originally dug to support a wall made up of side-by-side upright timbers. Like the south palisade uncovered in previous seasons, the curved narrow trench had straight sides, a flat bottom, and was barely wide enough for the upright logs to fit within. The curved trench fill also held similar dark stains of the long since decayed logs and around them a similar mixture of dark organic topsoil and chunks of subsoil clay. Putting up the palisade in a trench dug through the topsoil into the clay then packing that mixed dirt back around the logs would leave the type of dirt signature found. But unlike the south wall line, the bulwark palisade trench did not penetrate very far into subsoil, hardly deep enough to support upright timbers. The trench ranged from 5" deep, where it was cut by the foundation of the 1922 Pocahontas monument base, to ½" deep at a point near the river bank where grading wiped it away. The south line also lacked depth, disappearing as it approached the river bank. It is therefore likely that along and close to the old river bank, considerable original soil is missing, perhaps 2½' or

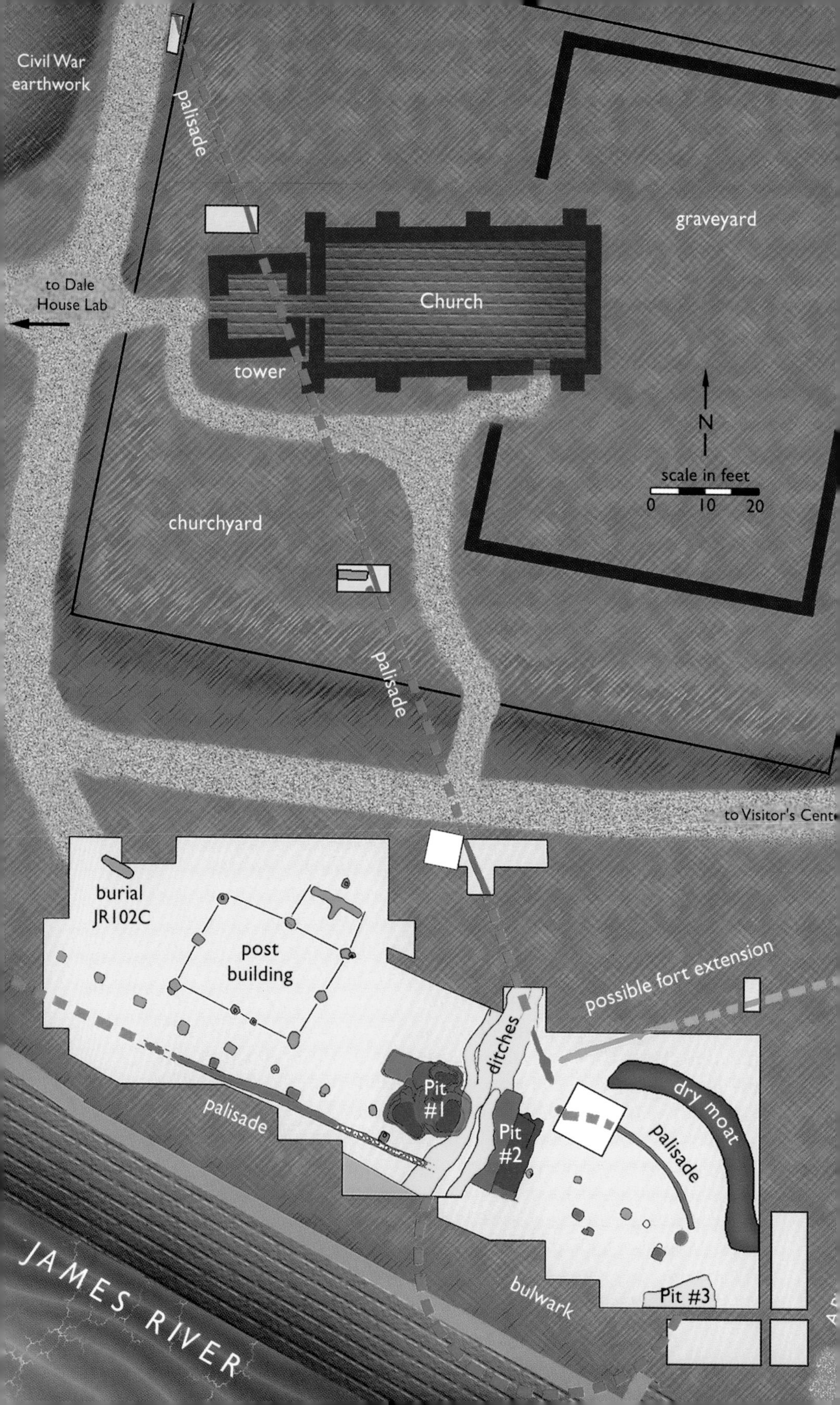

Civil War earthwork
palisade
graveyard
to Dale House Lab
Church
tower
N
scale in feet
0
10
20
churchyard
palisade
to Visitor's Cent
burial JR102C
post building
possible fort extension
ditches
Pit #1
Pit #2
dry moat
palisade
palisade
bulwark
Pit #3
JAMES RIVER

more. Yet all along the south edge of the site the plowzone soil became increasingly deeper above the clay subsoil, while along the upper section of the curved palisade trench, what appeared to be old topsoil actually survived below the plowed soil. The palisade trench cut through this layer establishing that this was close to the original ground surface when the palisade was constructed. The palisade trench itself held only Indian pottery, further evidence that it was erected on historically virgin ground (1607).

Actually the apparently confusing thick plowzone and survival of old topsoil can be explained, if an earth wall or a rampart once stood over and along the curved palisade. That is where the dirt went that came out of the nearby entrenchment. This bank also provided the approximately 2½' of soil necessary to support the palisade logs. Digging and piling up such an entrenchment-rampart would be standard procedure in fort construction, the idea being that an attacking enemy would have to struggle through the entrenchment and scale the rampart before even getting to the palisade. In any event, that dirt bank explains the survival of original topsoil below the depth of the James Fort earthwork. The bank kept the plow blade above the old topsoil even as the plowing gradually leveled the earthwork. In other words, the later plowing, perhaps as much as 150 years in duration, gradually took down the bank until it reached the old topsoil level and the last few inches of the palisade trench. Fortunately for the survival of the bulwark footprint, acquisition of the property by the APVA in 1893 ended cultivation of the area. This, however, does not explain why grading erased not only the topsoil but the palisade trenches along the riverbank.

Captain William Allen owned and farmed Jamestown Island during the middle of the 19th century. At his own expense, he had his slaves build an earthwork that the Confederate Army planned to use to help stop Union ships from sailing up the James and capturing Richmond. The surviving earthwork from that shore battery is still imposing, with some banks standing as high as 12' above the original pre-battery grade. The question is, where did the dirt come from for its construction? The likely answer is from along the nearby river bank. Some of James Fort dirt then is in the banks of the Confederate fort. In fact, there are reports that during the Civil War, fort builders found old burials and 17th-century armor. It also makes military sense to grade the eroded cliff down to water level, effectively eliminating cover for any Union amphibious landings. Pre-Civil War drawings of the church tower area clearly show dirt mounds, possibly left from James Fort and the cliff before Allen's slaves apparently graded it away.

Figure 12. Somewhat fanciful painting of Jamestown church tower area before the disruptive construction of the Civil War earthwork nearby.

The Civil War grading theory is all the more plausible when considering that only a few inches remain of the postholes inside the palisade trench, again strongly suggesting dirt is missing. These postholes seem to form an arc inside the palisade line. It is possible that they supported a wooden platform for mounting cannon.

Not perfectly concentric to the palisade, the entrenchment or dry moat is more "banana shaped" in plan with a definite terminus on the northwest end near the Pocahontas monument at a place where one could predict the curved palisade ended at a gate. Near the end of the bulwark trench, another dark line in the soil, actually found during the first few months of the digging, took on renewed significance. This stain extended only a few feet northwest where it disappeared at the edge of a series of 17th-century drainage ditches. In light of the pattern of the bulwark, the stain was finally identified as another palisade line emerging from the bulwark at a 46° angle to the south palisade line. This began to define the triangular James Fort. Additional excavations along that same alignment toward the church established that this palisade extended at least 210' where excavations ended for the season.

Removal of the fill in the dry moat revealed its original uneven depth, how it was dug, and that it was filled with hundreds of artifacts. The dry moat near the monument was the deepest, containing various layers of dirt that told the story of its life. At the bottom, rain-washed clay and decayed plant material slumped in from the rampart side as top layers of clay on the bank washed back in (see Fig. 13). Then organic topsoil-like fill, alternating with mixed soil containing small lumps of subsoil clay, filled the top of the dry moat, the mixture of dirt resulting from the partial leveling of the rampart when the fort was abandoned (natural washed clay would not produce lumps but shoveled soil would). As the natural erosion levels built up, glassmakers evidentially poured a hot layer of slag (waste produced during glass production) at the northwest end of the dry moat. The glass waste spilled in from the north and, being near the gate, it is logical to assume that a load of the material came from the manufacturing site inside the fort, through the gate, and then spilled into the partially open ditch. Since glassmaking was moved off the Island to Glasshouse Point in 1609 and the glassmakers arrived in 1608 when they made a trial of glass to be sent home, the slag deposit shows that the entrenchment was open long enough to accumulate eroded silt between May 1607 and 1608.[13] Other evidence that glassmakers worked in the vicinity of the bulwark existed in the bulwark backfill: high fired stoneware crucibles with glass adhering to their bowls and fine river sand filled the top of the center section of the backfilled entrenchment; possibly leftover raw material from the glassmaking process.

The excavation of the fill along the dry moat exposed two episodes of digging and backfilling: a later one extending the trench south, then, added to that, a right angle trench to the east. To confuse all this even more, another trench was dug into the right angle trench fill extending to the south. Whatever the time sequence, both of the earlier ditches could well have stood open and then been abandoned at about the same time. Or perhaps different crews were digging parts of the dry moat at the same time and eventually met slightly out of line with each other. It is possible too that the backfilling of these trenches took place at a slightly later time, yet all were still open at the same time and therefore part of the same bulwark. In any case, it is obvious from this that reading the architectural pages of the earth without hard foundations often is more an art than a science!

Figure 13. View of cross sections through the fill in a section of the dry moat, showing layers of washed clay at the bottom and backfill above.

To the south of the dry moat, where the clay below the plowzone begins to drop from the Civil War grading, additional digging showed that the subsoil surface once sloped even more toward the south, forming a drop off. Removal of the fill in one of the construction trenches from the 1907 seawall construction revealed deep 17th-century artifact-bearing soil. So far excavations only tested this disturbed area, but even with that limited information, it appears that the river eroded the original bank and the southern section of the bulwark. Then dirt rich with discarded animal bones and "trash"(a town landfill?) filled the erosion scar sometime after 1638, the date of a coin found in that layer. It appears that whatever removed the soil also destroyed the southern two thirds of the palisade trench and perhaps the outer entrenchment, although excavations are incomplete in that area. In any case, it is clear that the curved palisade line, the concentric ditch, and probably at least three large interior postholes represent the remains of the southeast bastion of James Fort. Also, the partial digging of fill along the sloping subsoil to the south uncovered what seems to be a large pit of yet unknown extent, which contained copper and military objects similar in nature to the clay Pit I. Two copper Irish pennies (1602) came from that fill.

From the beginning, our plan for the excavation was to start at point "A" and progress to point "B" then "C" and so on, continuously connecting 10' square to 10' square as our discoveries led us. The spot testing and trenching of the 1930s, '40s, and '50s were very different. That work certainly learned much about greater Jamestown, but the buildings and other parts of the town were disconnected in time and space. The lesson from those earlier explorations was clear: we needed a full view of a large area in order to "connect" whatever new things might turn up. This was the only chance we had to understand a continuous footprint of something the size of James Fort. Once the basic lines of the fort became clear, leaps of faith could be made. The known angle of the north palisade was a perfect basis to correctly guess its course. Thus four separate tests were made along the north line, two south of and two north of the reconstructed church.

Excavation first ventured to a place predicted to be beyond the disturbances of the town drainage ditches northwest of the south bulwark gate. The palisade line survived there directly in line as it did in all of the four tests! There was also an effort to determine whether or not a dry moat existed to the east of the palisade, as it did paralleling the bulwark. The additional digging uncovered another larger and deeper trench, but it was not parallel to the pali-

Figure 14. View of test trench south of the 1907 reconstructed church showing: section of north palisade trench line (1); original undisturbed topsoil (2); brick and mortar from the destruction and excavation of the church 1896-1906 (3).

3
2
1

Figure 15. Test excavation along the north base of the original 17th-century church tower (left) uncovered original unplowed Jamestown ground levels above a perfectly preserved north wall palisade trench containing distinct marks of the decayed upright timber (above).

sade line. However, the fill contained the same mixture of prehistoric and early historic artifacts found in the palisades, suggesting that it was filled during the same early time period. That being the case, the trench may be a remnant of some expansion of the original fort, but precisely in what way it added to the plan could not be determined by this small excavated area.

The first trench proved that a palisade line predated the town ditches that cut through it and that the line extended toward the churchyard. The next test along the projected track near the church uncovered not only another run of the palisade line but what appeared to be a related posthole, where a support post once stood. That was the same construction technique found along the south curtain. This section of the line struck an alignment that obviously was heading toward the center of the church tower, the only above ground remnant of original Jamestown. This, of course, places the brick church foundations east of and presumably outside the fort. So much for the theory that churches never change locations. At any rate, the two tests north of the tower strongly suggest that the tower was built directly on the site of the abandoned palisade line at exactly 150' from the southeast bulwark. If Strachey's 300' curtain dimension is accurate, then for some reason, the tower was built exactly at the center of the eastern fort wall.

The traces of the palisade near the north side of the tower were the most vividly preserved of the line. Timber impressions were clearly visible in the small section uncovered. Like the other trenches in the yard, it was clear that this was unplowed ground which meant that some of the original ground surface of James Fort lay there undisturbed since 1607. It is important to note that the palisade trench is much deeper here. Apparently, respect for the burials in the churchyard kept the church grounds from being plowed and graded since the 17th century. Thus the original grade survives, protecting the complete palisade ditch below it.

A small test was also made further along the projected palisade line, just outside the iron churchyard fence where the grade drops to the gravel road that passes in front of the church. The grading necessary to put in and maintain the road should have left a cross section of the palisade on the bank next to the graded surface. That proved to be wrong, as the dirt creating the bank appears to be fill brought to level the churchyard inside its iron gate around 1907. The test appeared to be even more of a failure after it uncovered two deep electrical lines in a trench along the concrete curb of the road. However, removal of that modern fill in a small test hole uncovered a heavy layer of burned wood immediately below the wires. Finally, digging below the charcoal revealed more of the palisade trench. Not only is it clear that the palisade trench line survived destruction during utility line installation and road grading, but the combination of charcoal above the palisade presents the possibility that debris from the fire of January 1608 exists undisturbed in this area as well.

Completely revealing the burial JR102C was among the major revelations of 1996, but suspicion arose that the rectangular dark stain was a burial during the 1995 season. Realizing the painstaking detail and specialized knowledge required for the investigation of human burials, the excavation was postponed until experts were available for the work. Excavations proceeded when Smithsonian Institution forensic anthropologist, Dr. Douglas Owsley, became available in the fall. Soon the outline of decayed coffin boards and nails appeared only 2' below the present ground surface. Again the shaft fill indicated a burial very early in the settlement, perhaps as early as 1607. For such an ancient internment, the skeleton turned out to be relatively intact. Details of the burial are discussed previously (see page 1).

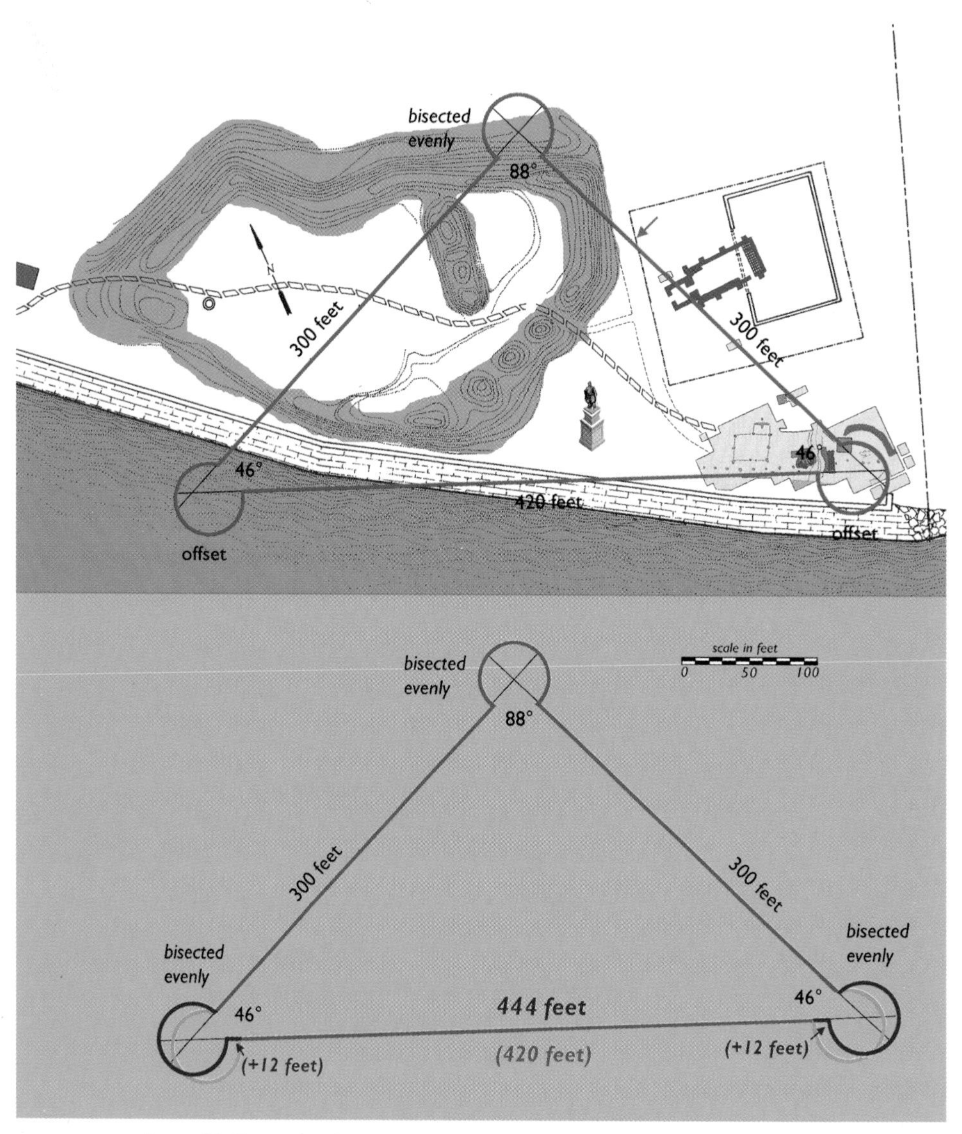

Figure 16. The predicted original position of James Fort in the Civil War/sea wall/church area (top), based on open excavation at the south corner of the fort and tests along the east wall line. The diagram below the map shows how the archaeologically discovered asymmetry of the reconstructed bastion circle would shortened the south wall line enough to match exactly Strachey's measurement of 1609-10.

James Fort Rediscovered

What of the above evidence builds the case for the discovery of James Fort? First, the survival of the two palisade walls or curtains defines a triangle. Log impressions indicate the walls were something more than a fence, which is also suggested by the existence of the intermittent support posts. Moreover, the palisade trenches are over 2' deep in unplowed or ungraded areas. It is also extremely significant that these two walls are at an angle to each other reflecting both Percy's and Smith's descriptions of 1607 and 1608. Perhaps more telling is that the two lines form a 46 degree angle, which matches William Strachey's 300' x 300' x 420' triangle, if the bulwarks were as far off center at the angles as the southeast bulwark indicates. The palisade line runs to, and likely under, the church tower, the oldest above ground architectural ruin at Jamestown. It is true that the first reference to a brick church comes no earlier than 1639, but it is possible that the tower, which is presumed a later addition to the 1639 church, may in fact pre-date that later building. Because of the loopholes (slot openings for firing) in the walls of the third story and because the tower seems to be at the center of Strachey's 300' curtain, it is possible the structure served as a watchtower for the "five square" Jamestown first described by Smith in 1608.[14] In fact, a section of palisade found extending at a right angle from north of the east bulwark gate might be part of that expanded plan; that is, part of a square eastern palisaded area added to the existing triangle. The ash layer found overlaying the east palisade is perhaps an area

Figure 17. This apparent triangular fort in Belgium of ca. 1640 seems to offer a remarkable comparision to the eyewitness descriptions of faraway James Fort.

hardest hit by the fire of January 1608, as well. In any event, the curtain palisades are the oldest construction on the site.

In order for these palisades to not be parts of some kind of triangular fence line, they need to form a logical fort plan, especially if it matches eye witness descriptions and sketches. It must have bulwarks at "each corner." Certainly the curved palisade ditch and its concentric entrenchment conform to such a plan. It is unlikely that any other type of a palisaded enclosure would have these characteristics. Only one quarter of the east bulwark survives, but it would have enclosed a circle about 50' in diameter. This would be enough space for cannon in each bulwark described by Smith with a proper recoil distance.

And what may be even more telling than these details is the relative offset position of the reconstructed circle vis-à-vis the curtain walls. This meant that the bulwark extends its greatest distance toward the river. That makes sense according to directions in a 16th-century "how-to-build-forts" manual. Since, according to the directions, the water on the south of James Fort gave the defenses an advantage in that direction, the curtain on that side was supposed to be the longest and the bulwarks the "sharpest".[15] Now if the other southern bulwark is equally oriented more to the south and the north bulwark oriented symmetrically to equally cover the east and west curtains, then the south wall becomes shorter than the angles would describe, short enough to match Strachey's dimension exactly.

Further, the evidence for James Fort is even stronger yet because of the types and age of the artifacts found along with its footprint. The dating of the various parts of the fort based on the objects found with them establish the earliest possible date for its construction. And the objects clearly show that the occupation was military. The bulwark dry moat fill produced the breastplate; a small shield known as a buckler; the iron entrenching tool, presumably for digging the narrow and deep palisade trenches; and the Border ware drinking jug, all as old as 1607, and all likely used by soldiers. Certainly the industrial waste, mixed with the military things, show that the craftsmen among the early colonists were hard at work making Algonquian jewelry to trade and conducting glass experiments and other metallurgical activities for the Virginia Company enterprise. Iron smelting, black smithing, and brick-making were also present and necessary for economic and physical survival those first three years.

Figure 18. Complete breastplate being excavated from the dry moat.

Figure 19. Glass slag and an intact Border ware drinking jug in the dry moat.

Figure 20. The palisade trench at the south bulwark and a special 17th-century entrenching tool found in the dry moat, undoubtedly used by soldiers and laborers to create it.

by Nicholas Lucckettti

Chapter 2

"Some Island That Is Strong By Nature"

Now that there is convincing archaeological evidence of the location and, to a great extent, the character of James Fort, a re-examination of the questions of *why James Fort was built where it was and the way it was?* seems in order. Of course, many things influenced the colonists' decision of where and how to build James Fort such as: who the enemy was or, perhaps more importantly, who they *thought* the enemy was; their earlier English military and colonial experiences; their instructions from the sponsor of the expedition, the Virginia Company of London; guidance from their military manuals; and the lay of the land. The artifacts found in the excavation, primarily parts of armor, weapons, and ammunition with few domestic objects, emphasize the military nature of the first settlement. As such, that is the best perspective to view the first years of the Jamestown colony.

Enemies

The English must have known that, sooner or later, they would clash with the Virginia Indians living along the James River. What the English did not know until after they landed was that most of the tribes of coastal Virginia were part of a chiefdom governed by a supreme ruler, Powhatan. Even before the arrival of the first Jamestown colonists, the Powhatan tribes of the Hampton Roads area had a substantial history of less than friendly contacts with

Figure 21. Detail of John Smith's Map of Virginia *showing "The new fort" and the Paspahegh village of Mattapanient.*

Europeans. One well known episode was the short-lived Spanish Jesuit mission established somewhere between the James and York rivers in 1570. It was wiped out after only 3 months by the local Indians.[16] In 1603, Captain Bartholomew Gilbert and three sailors were killed by Indians on Virginia's Eastern Shore.[17] And surely the tribes of the Powhatan chiefdom knew of the fighting that erupted in 1585-1587 between the Roanoke Island settlers and neighboring Indians.[18] These and other hostilities may explain the greeting the Jamestown colonists received when they landed at Cape Henry in April of 1607. They were attacked by either Chesapeake or Nansemond Indians who, according to George Percy, "with their bows in their mouths, charged us very desparately in their faces," and wounded Captain Gabriel Archer and a sailor.[19] And although the first meeting with the Kecoughtan Indians at Point Comfort was peaceful,[20] just two weeks after settling at Jamestown Island, a large force from Paspahegh, the nearest Indian village to Jamestown Island, attacked the newborn settlement, killing two and wounding ten.[21]

But the primary peril that preoccupied Elizabethan England was their archenemy, Spain. Little wonder then that, despite a peace treaty signed by the two countries in 1604, the rising tide of animosity and distrust that arose during the 1500s spilled over into the next century. Indeed, the instructions given to the first colonists cautioned, "And to the end That You not be Surprised as the French were in Florida by Melidus...."[22] The reference is to Pedro Menendez, Governor of St. Augustine, who routed the French in a surprise attack on Fort Caroline in 1565.[23] English settlement in the New World was a continuing source of irritation to Spain, who vehemently protested that it was in violation of the treaty. Don Pedro de Zuniga, Spain's ambassador to London from July 1605 to May 1610, consistently urged Philip II to destroy the fledgling Virginia colony[24] and, in fact, the Spanish Council of War planned to attack Jamestown every year from 1607-1617.[25]

The specter of the Spanish threat continually haunted the Jamestown settlers. Only a few months after arriving at Jamestown Island, John Smith reported that Captain George Kendall was executed for instigating a rebellion, possibly inspired by his Catholic, and therefore Spanish, sympathies.[26] In 1609, Smith believed two of the Jamestown colonists, "the Dutchman and one Bently," were involved in a Spanish plot to lead the Indians in an attack on the colonists.[27] The same year, a Spanish spy ship made its way from St. Augustine to the Chesapeake Bay, endeavoring to pinpoint Jamestown and determine how best to attack it. Another Spanish intelligence voyage, commanded by Captain Diego de

Molina, took place in 1611. Molina and two others were taken prisoner and Molina remained in Virginia until 1616, all the time smuggling out letters in the soles of a Venetian merchant's shoe.[28] Even as late as 1620, the well known John Rolfe wrote about the arrival of a Dutch man-of-war whose captain warned of an impending Spanish attack on Virginia.[29] Despite all the rancor and provocations, the Spanish never attacked Jamestown.

Lessons of Foreign Wars and the Lost Colonies

Virginia Company officials surely heeded lessons learned from earlier English military and colonizing campaigns in developing plans for their sponsorship of the Jamestown settlement. During the late 16th and early 17th centuries, England was engaged in two major land conflicts: the colonization of Ireland and campaigns in the Low Countries where English troops were supporting the Dutch Estates General in their revolt against Catholics and Spain. In the New World, the English learned about colonization the hard way through their abortive attempts to establish settlements in Canada in the 1560s, North Carolina in the 1580s, and later exploratory voyages to the North Carolina Outer Banks and the Chesapeake Bay.

Elizabethan colonization in Ireland began in the 1560s. This effort escalated to conquest in the late 16th century, accompanied

Figure 22. Sixteenth-century engraving of the English army on the march in Ireland.

Figure 23. Eighty Years' War fortified village northeast of Leiden, Netherlands, 1575.

by the deployment of English troops. The Irish, who had virtually no artillery and relatively few firearms, fought principally with guerrilla tactics: hit-and-run skirmishes, ambushes, and general harassment of the enemy. English soldiers were frustrated,

> *because [the Irish] are only trained to skimish upon bogs and difficult passes or passages of woods, and not to stand or fight in a firm body upon the plains, they think it no shame to fly or run off from fighting, as they advantage.*[30]

and

> *[the Irish soldiers] never making good any fight, but bogering with his shot and flying from bush to bush...they hold no dishonour to run away; for the best sconce and castle for their security is their feet.*[31]

In marked contrast to the Elizabethan-Irish conflict were the wars in the Low Countries. In 1584, the leader of the Dutch Revolt, William the Silent, was assassinated. The alarmed Dutch Estate General sought outside help against the Spanish by negotiating a treaty with Queen Elizabeth. The Queen dispatched an English army to the Netherlands that remained there until 1604, when King James I made peace with Philip II of Spain. That war involved major engagements with large numbers of troops, cavalry, extensive use of artillery, and sophisticated offensive operations. Professional military engineers constructed massive and complex state-of-the-art fortifications which, in contrast to the guerrilla fighting in Ireland, fostered extensive siege warfare.

It is logical to assume that engagement in major European military campaigns by the English taught them the latest military science, but their tradition in fort construction evidently was not as evolved as that of their Continental neighbors:

> *...which practise [of fortification], although it be not so common amongst us, (or of some thought altogether so necessary for us) as for the nations whise countries do lie adjoying together, where an enemie may enter with a great number of horse & men upon the sodaine....*[32]

and

> *Architecture military...as have more fully handled this subject in other Languages. But considering how little hath beene written hereof in our English tongue, and that the practice of it with us is very rare.*[33]

Perhaps the English experience that was most relevant to the Virginia Company enterprise was Sir Walter Raleigh's attempts in 1585 and 1587 to establish a colony at Roanoke Island in North Carolina. Although unsuccessful, Raleigh's efforts were tantamount to an outdoor seminar, educating the English to a new, and frequently harsh, environment, one that was quite similar to that which John Smith and his comrades would find later at Jamestown Island.

Initially, Raleigh sent a reconnaissance voyage to the Outer Banks in 1584 that actually returned to England with Manteo and Wanchese, two local Croatoan Indians who apparently volunteered for the mission. This undoubtedly gave the English detailed knowledge of Algonquian Indian culture in the region. One year later, Raleigh sent 108 men and boys, commanded by Ralph Lane, to set up a base on the Outer Banks. Roanoke Island was chosen as the site for the colony, in large measure to hide from Spanish detection. Within months hostilities broke out between the local Indians and the English, resulting in the beheading of the local chief, Wingina. The Lane colony returned to England in 1586 and a belated supply fleet left a holding party of 15 men, who were later driven from the island by an Indian attack. Governor John White established a second colony of 117 men, women, and children at Roanoke Island in 1587. White soon sailed for England for supplies, but the threat to England from the Spanish Armada delayed his return until 1590. Upon his return, he found an abandoned wooden fort and cottages. The people were gone, eventually becoming known as the legendary "Lost Colony."[34]

Advice given to the Lane colony, probably written by a professional English soldier, required a force five times the size of the 1585 colony to build a fortification strong enough to stand up against the Spanish as follows:

For Master Rauleys Viage

...yett will I have furnytur to prevent the Invasion of the Spanyardes.

Of this nomber I would dayly have...500, men to labor for the buldyng of your forte.

...What maner of forte I woulde have, I would have It a pentangell in this manner. With, v, large bulwarkes the Casemates of the Boulwarkes large and open, with a way out of the bulwarke and an other Into the Streat. The Collionsides or ocrechons, large and longe, The Curtyns sumwhat slant, that the yearthe may lye the faster and the rampir of the Curtyns very braude, Every bulwarke shall have bye It a cavalir to beat the feald, or tow wer better,...The diche I would have large

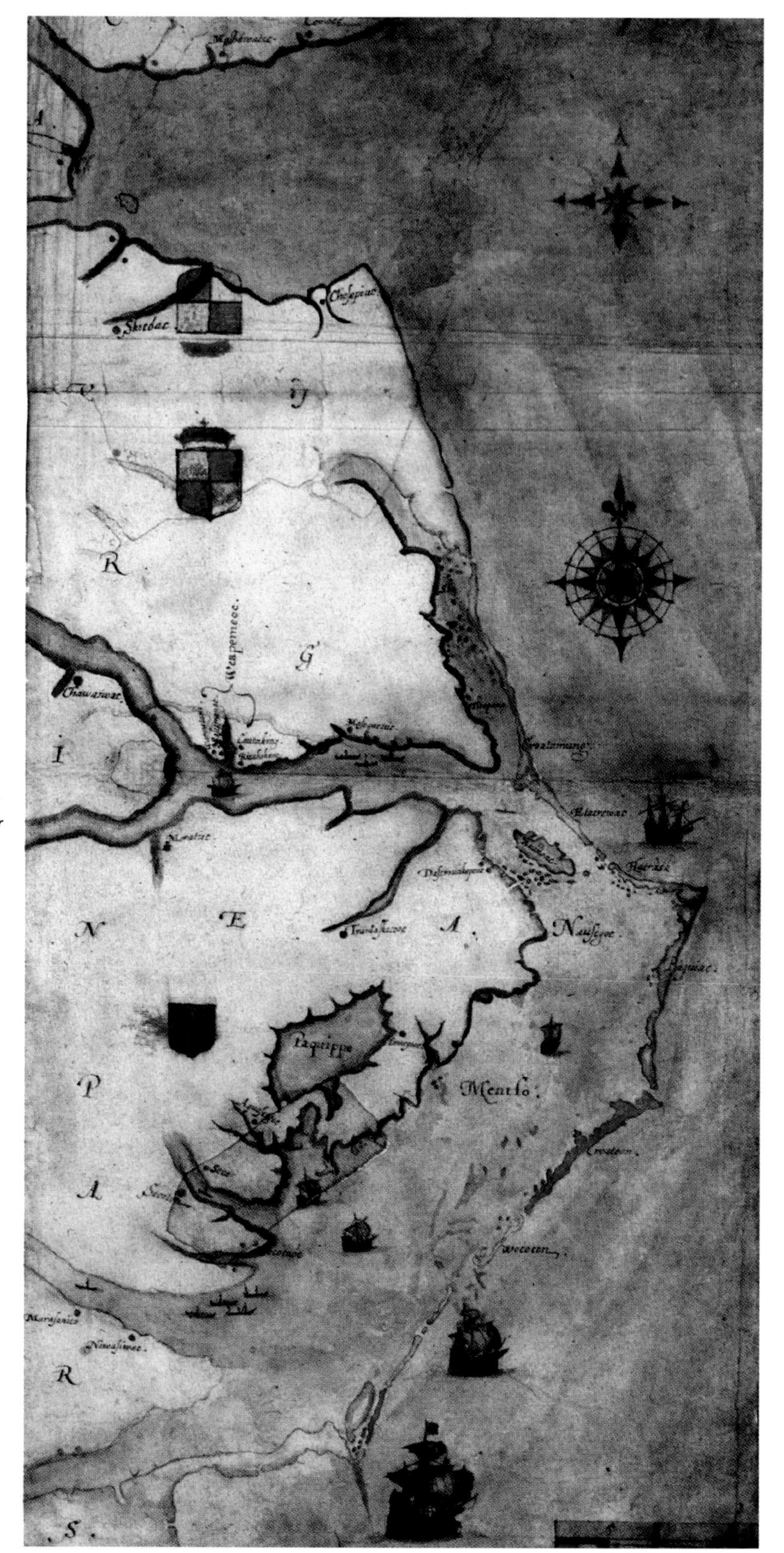

Figure 24. John White's Map of Raleigh's Virginia *depicting detailed information of the lower Cheaspeake Bay and the Outer Banks.*

with walles beyond the diche a 20 foot from the diche I would have a wall of, 4. Foot hyght with arayll on the tope so as the tope of this wall shouldbe within a 3 foot as hyght as the parrepett of my Curtyns or bulwarkes. Within the diche I would have a hyght pall of xv foot hyght by Cause It shall prevent any suddeyn Scallado, for that youre forte is of yearthe, which yow know in tyme moulders. This forte with 500, men with the help and Incorragment of the Commander wilbe finished In a monthe. Which being fynyshed I know no reason but it is abell long to hould a gaynst all the forces of Indda. How I would have It seated, eyther uppon rocke, marrishe, an Island or peninsulla....[35]

Obviously the 104 men of the initial Jamestown settlement would have to build something less than ideal.

The Roanoke ventures left a paradoxical legacy. They provided a new awareness of the Virginia coastal environment, both natural and cultural, and at the same time, initiated an enduring record of distrust and enmity between the English and the Native Americans.[36] Although John White is the only known survivor of the Lost Colony, several of the principals involved in the Roanoke ventures were around in the years leading up to Jamestown—Sir Walter Raleigh, Thomas Hariot, Ralph Lane, and Sir Richard Grenville, among the most prominent. They surely passed along their New World insights in some way to the Virginia Company. Nonetheless, the limited number of Jamestown settlers were incapable of building a fort in the manner outlined by the Lane instructions. Their solution, however, was to locate small "lookout" forts where Spanish ships would have to approach from the ocean. From there, guards could warn the main defense upriver at Jamestown Island.

Theory And Practice

In 1589, Paule Ive, an English veteran of the Low Countries wars, wrote the following:

The delineation of a fort that shall serve for a royall frontier, the figure triangular is not to be used at all, nor the quadrant, but only on those watrie grounds where it can not be approached, neither is the cinqueangle to be chosen for any perfection that is in ye figure, for this purpose (although that many god forts are made in that forme of the Castle of Antwerp, the citadel of Turyne and others) but rather for sparing of charges in building and mainteing the fort. Where water may be found, the fort may be the lesse,

Figure 25. A 1562 French settlement of Charles Fort in modern day South Carolina.

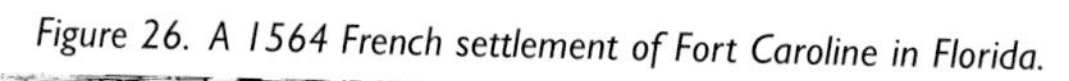

Figure 26. A 1564 French settlement of Fort Caroline in Florida.

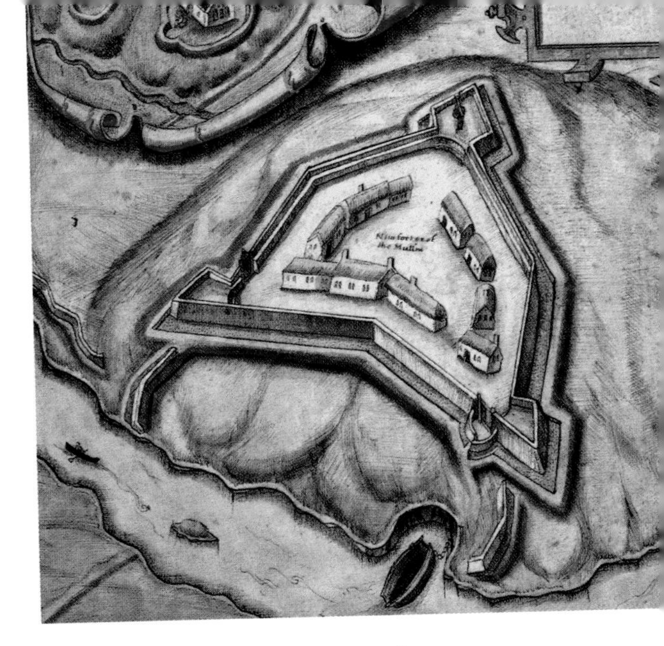

Figure 27. Illustration of 1601 English fort on the Blackwater River in Northern Ireland.

> *and needeth not the ditches so deepe as in dry ground, for it will be free from surprise, skale, and myning, and being battered the assault will be troublesome, for that one man standing upon firme ground may resist five upon a bridge, beat, floate, or such like. Moreover, the fort standing neere unto any river, may receive great commodities of it for the bringing of things necessary unto it, both for making and mainteining of it.*[37]

Ive seems to advise against building triangular forts altogether except along waterways. Accordingly, the frontier French forts at Charles Fort on Parris Island, South Carolina (1562), and Fort Caroline (1564) on the St. John's River in Florida were triangular, as was one of the first forts built by the Spanish at St. Augustine, Florida. English forces also constructed a triangle-like fort in Northern Ireland in 1601. All of these forts had comparatively small garrisons, which could more quickly and easily build and protect a triangular-shaped defense.

There are two archaeologically recorded earthen fortifications that may be helpful in understanding the design of James Fort. In 1950, J.C. Harrington excavated the remains of what he believed was a 16th-century earthwork at Fort Raleigh National Historic Site on Roanoke Island. Harrington's excavations revealed a "star-shaped" defense defined by a surrounding trench or dry moat.[38] Archaeological excavations also uncovered a similarly sized but linear trench at the site of John Smith's 1609 fort across the river from Jamestown Island in present day Surry County (see fig. 21, "The new fort").[39] The Smith's Fort and Fort Raleigh earthworks suggest the size of trenches necessary to create defenses that were largely earthen ramparts, likely with palisades on top.

Figure 28. Aerial view of reconstructed earthwork at Fort Raleigh.

Settlement Instructions

The Jamestown adventurers were given instructions from the Virginia Company of London to be opened when they arrived in Virginia. They read in part:

> *When it shall please God to Send you on the Coast of Virginia you shall Do your best Endeavor to find out a Safe port in the Entrance of Some navigable River making Choose of Such a one as runt furthest into the Land.*
>
> *...first Let Captain Newport Discover how far that River may be found navigable that you may make Election of the Strongest most Fertile and wholesome place....*
>
> *...you may perchance find a hundred miles from the Rivers mouth and the farther up the better for if you sit Down near the Entrance Except it be in Some Island that is Strong by nature An Enemy that may approach you on Even Ground may Easily pull You Out and if he be Driven to Seek You a hundred miles within the Land in boats you shall from both sides of your River where it is Narrowest So beat them with Your muskets as they shall never be Able to prevail Against You.*
>
> *...you shall Do Well to make this Double provision first Erect a Little Sconce at the Mouth of the River that may Lodge Some ten men With Whom you Shall Leave a boat that when any fleet shall be in Sight they may Come with Speed to Give You Warning. Secondly, you must in no Case Suffer any of the natural people of the Country to inhabit between You and the Sea Coast....*[40]

A primary concern recurring throughout the instructions is security: "find out a Safe port"; "make Election of the Strongest" with strongest taking precedence over fertile and wholesome; and "Some Island that is Strong by nature." Crucial to establishing a defensible settlement was controlling the entrance "at the Mouth of the River," an urgency the Jamestown colonists also recognized,

> *...In the mouth of this River three Ys a place so fortified by nature, That If the Spaniard who will start upon this alarm, Recover this place before Vs, this action Ys utterly overthrown....*[41]

It didn't take long for the colonists to place a garrison at the entrance to the James River at Point Comfort that would signal the initial alert and provide the first line of defense against European intruders:

> *Upon Point Comfort our men did the last year [1608] (as you have heard) raise a little fortification, which since hath been better perfected and is likely to prove a strong fort and is now kept by Captain James Davis with forty men, and hath to name Algernon Fort....*[42]

Aside from the construction of Fort Algernon, the colonists failed to comply with the Virginia Company's instructions if they are read literally, but perhaps they were meant only for general guidance. After all, how could merchants, officials, or even military advisers write specific directives when there was no detailed knowledge of the James River area until it was explored in 1607? Certainly had they been more familiar with the region, they would not have advised the colonists to settle somewhere where there were no Indians living between them and the ocean, which was impossible.

The Virginia Company also hoped that the settlement could be built "a hundred miles from the Rivers mouth and the farther up the better," but Jamestown Island is only 36 miles from the mouth of the river. Nevertheless, that distance was sufficient to provide ample warning time. Under ideal winds and tide, it took a 17th-century ship 6 or 7 hours to reach Jamestown Island once it passed Point Comfort. However, these conditions are quite infrequent and it is much more common for the trip to take nearly a day,[43] allowing plenty of time for the advance sentinels to warn Jamestown of approaching hostile ships.

Jamestown Island

The low, marshy, bug-ridden Jamestown Island seems to modern judgment the worst possible place for the colonists to choose for their Virginia base. But to the military mind of the Elizabethan/Jacobean period it made perfect sense. There are a number of natural positions between the Island and the Atlantic that protect the Island from attack coming up river. Again, the fort at Point Comfort provided deterrence and advance warning, as did Hog Island, about three miles downstream from Jamestown Island. The Jamestown colonists took advantage of this position, fortifying Hog Island with a blockhouse sometime before 1609, "...to give us notice of any shipping."[44] Additionally, Jamestown Island is screened from any ships coming upriver by Hog Island, which in turn has a clear line-of-sight to the mouth of the James River. A lookout perched in a 20 foot high blockhouse could see the tall masts of even a relatively small ship 16 miles away.[45] And, in 1607, Jamestown Island was an isthmus, connected to the mainland by a narrow neck that could be easily protected by a blockhouse, which was built by 1609. Further, Jamestown Island is composed of a series of marshes and ridges, and one ridge on the western end of the island is well suited for fortification. It is both the highest piece of ground on the river side of Jamestown Island and is naturally protected from approaching enemies by low ground on the east and west and a marsh to the north.

Although the James River is wide, navigation is limited to a narrow channel which meanders from side-to-side as it moves up river. The channel is closer to shore at the western end of Jamestown Island than at any other point downriver, and George Percy indicated that this was the deciding factor in establishing the town there.[46] While the channel allowed convenient anchorage for ships at the western end of the Island, elsewhere it kept enemy vessels conveniently offshore. The distance from the western end of Jamestown Island to the south shore of the river is little more than a mile, and it is the narrowest point along the river from Jamestown Island to Hampton Roads. As a last line of defense, the channel would force any enemy ships that managed to make it upriver to sail within the range of the town's artillery. John Smith reports that Jamestown had "four and twentie peeces of Ordnance of Culvering, Demiculvering, Sacar, and Falcon," and "most well mounted upon convenient plat-formes."[47] At that time a culverin had an extreme range of over a mile at 6750 feet,[48] well beyond the James River channel from the western ridge. Thus, even if an enemy ship with heavier guns reached Jamestown Island, it could

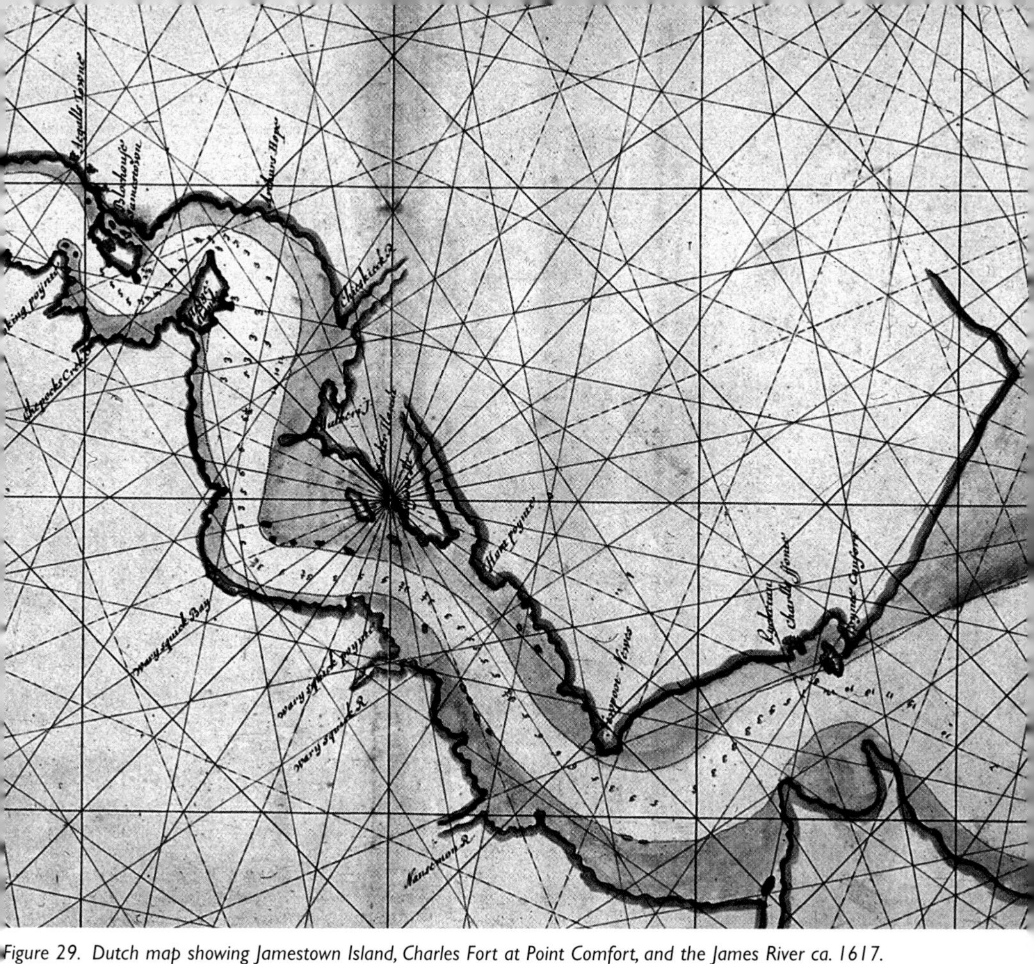

Figure 29. Dutch map showing Jamestown Island, Charles Fort at Point Comfort, and the James River ca. 1617.

not engage in an artillery battle outside of the reach of Jamestown's culverin, nor could it get close enough to the western ridge to fire point blank at a fort.

While the Spanish may have been the foremost foe as they sailed to Virginia, the settlers knew from the first day they landed at Cape Henry that the Virginia Indians were a real threat to their survival. So Jamestown Island was not only a good strategic choice against attack from the Spanish, but it provided a perfect location to protect the colonists from the local Powhatans. Accordingly, the expedition's leaders, it can be argued, made the best decision given the circumstances and resources. They built a fort sufficiently strong to protect themselves from guerrilla-type Virginia Indian warfare. They did not, and really could not, build a state-of-the-art Low Countries fortress that would repel the Spanish, which, in any case, may or may not ever show up. The triangular fort walls of small posts in narrow trenches were more than adequate to ward off Powhatan arrows. In fact, the proof of its success is that James Fort never fell to any enemy. [49]

Figure 30. Excavation of an iron semi-swept hilt from an early 17th-century rapier.

by Beverly Straube

Chapter 3

Arms, Armor, Medicine, Money, a Token, and a Jug

The *Jamestown Rediscovery* artifact collection numbers over 150,000 objects and is beginning to fill in the gaps in what we know of Jamestown's past. The artifacts establish *when* in time events happened and illustrate for the first time *what* types of objects made up the material world of the first years of Virginia settlement. These objects reflect trade among England, other countries, and the New World, patterns of warfare, day-to-day survival, wealth, and status in the early colony. We often cannot know of Jamestown in any more intimate way, as the written record of Jamestown's earliest years is scant and often contradictory.

Some of the objects found at the James Fort site that reveal the lifestyle of the early colonists include arms and armor, health and medicinal objects, the money the colonists had, and the pottery they used.

Arms and Armor

Reference is often made to the Virginia Company record of old armor, "unfitt for any moderne service," that was bestowed upon the colony by James I from his royal armory following the massacre of 1622.[50] Other documentary evidence has shown that this qualified generosity toward Jamestown is not singular to the king, but is a pattern that was begun by the Virginia Company itself. While the group of investors who were backing Jamestown appear to have been quite generous in supplying manpower for Virginia, they were equally stingy in provisioning these individuals once they had arrived. The records are full of requests from the colony, especially for food and clothing. As early as 1608 John Smith recounts the colony's problems in receiving adequate supplies "to get wherewith to live, and defend our selves against the inconstant Salvages."[51] In August 1611, George Percy writes to his brother in London that the colony's store is "affording no other meanes then a pound of meale a day and a little Oatmeale."[52] And, as late as May 1621, council member Captain Nuce complains to Sir Edwyn Sandy, treasurer of the Virginia Company, that "the half yeere, for wch onely we were victualled, since our landinge, is now almost expyred; sure I am, our provisions are expended, and yet wee here of no supplie."[53]

Some of the supplies acquired for Jamestown may, in fact, have been unused stores recycled from previous voyages. John Smith, for instance, is recorded as complaining four months after arrival in Virginia about the rotten tents they had to use.[54] Recent excavations have uncovered further indications of this practice. Leaden devices known as cloth seals have been excavated that were once clamped on fabrics manufactured in England under Elizabeth I's reign. These textiles would have been made at least four years before the founding of Jamestown, which is an unusually long time for this valuable commodity to remain unused.

Examples of obsolete military equipment supplied to Jamestown include a boss from a buckler and a breastplate uncovered during recent excavations. While they may be further examples of the Virginia Company's stinginess, there could be another reason for their presence at Jamestown. While outmoded for the type of formal battles common in Europe, they could represent arms and armor that were quite suitable for the ambush-type engagements the colonists encountered with the Virginia Indians. The Indians relied primarily on stealth and surprise in their attacks; and, with the accuracy of the bow and arrow falling sharply in distances over 50 yards, these skirmishes were at fairly short range.[55] The buckler was very well suited for hand-to-hand combat and especially useful in deflecting blows from the axes and clubs wielded by the Indians.

A buckler is a small leather shield used in England from the 13th through the 16th centuries. They are usually round, about 11-14" in diameter, and slightly concave toward the opponent. The buckler has a leather foundation which is reinforced with metal, and a central iron boss with a projecting spike. This iron boss is all that remains of the buckler found in James Fort. One side of it has been bashed in which may be a result of armed conflict. In combat, bucklers were used in the hand opposite the sword to "dint and blunt the edge of [the] Enemies Sword," and protect the wearer's body " from Blows and Wounds."[56]

The terms *shield*, *target*, and *buckler* may have been used interchangeably in the 17th century, even though they refer to devices of different sizes. A shield was large enough to provide shelter for a soldier as it stood upon the ground. A target was smaller and ovoid and strapped upon the forearm with two leather straps. The buckler was smaller still and held in the non-sword hand.

A 1622 record seems to be making a distinction in listing 500 "Targetts & Bucklers" among the "unserviceable" arms in the Tower of London available for the Virginia Company.[57] On the other hand, John Smith's claim to have once used his Indian guide

Figure 31. Iron central element or boss to a small hand-held shield known as a buckler (right). The buckler would have been made of leather with metal reinforcements. By the early 17th century, its use as a military weapon was dying out.

As seen in these two painting details, bucklers were standard arms carried by gentlemen and soldiers in the 16th century. At this time, "every servingman, from the base to the best, carried a buckler at his backe, which hung by the hilt or pomell of his sword which hung before him."

as a buckler best describes the forearm protection of a target. According to Smith's account, while under attack from 200 Indians, Smith bound the Indian "to his arme with his garters, and used him as a buckler." Smith survived to be taken prisoner with only a wound to the thigh but the fate of his hapless human shield is unknown![58]

By 1607, the buckler was considered an archaic weapon in England. The "poking fight of rapier and dagger" was to blame for the "dearth of sword and Buckler fight."[59] Italian fencing schools in the mid-16th century championed use of the long piercing blade of the rapier used in conjunction with a dagger in the non-sword hand to block thrusts. This technique gained widespread popularity among English swordsmen. The buckler provided little defense against the thrusts of the lengthy rapier and was abandoned by the 1570s.

While breastplates are not uncommon finds on early 17th-century Virginia sites, it is unusual to unearth one dating from the 15th century. This is when the breastplate recovered within the fort area was made, making it is the earliest example of plate armor excavated in Virginia.

Breastplates, protecting the chest area, were integral parts of armor worn from the 15th through the 17th centuries. Because they stylistically reflect male civilian clothing, they are easily datable. Early breastplates, like the one found in James Fort, were very rounded with a short bottom flange, mirroring the current fashion of the cloth doublet or jacket. Later, following changes in the doublet, the breastplate developed a pronounced central ridge, running from the neck to the waist, and the lines become elongated, forming a very pronounced "V" to the front. The ridge not only provides a glancing surface to the blow of a sword or pike, but is an interpretation in steel of the effect made by the row of tiny round brass buttons running down the front of the doublet. The high V-shaped bottom of the breastplate copied the cut of the doublet which accommodated the short puffy breeches that were then in vogue.

As already mentioned, the excavated breastplate is of the very rounded 15th-century type. The neck and underarm edges that would normally be rolled for the wearer's comfort show signs of being cut down. This has resulted in the breastplate being very narrow through the chest area, perhaps providing a better fit for the Jamestown soldier lucky enough to wear it.

Late 16th- or early 17th-century breastplate excavated at Jordan's Journey, Prince George County, Virginia (above) showing the pronounced ridge and V-shaped bottom.

Figure 32. Fifteenth-century breastplate (above) from James Fort. The knight in Albrecht Dürer's 1513 engraving (below) is wearing a breastplate with a similarly rounded profile.

Albrecht Dürer, German, 1471-1528, The Knight, Death and the Devil, engraving, 1513, 24.4 x 18.8 cm, Clarence Buckingham Collection, 1938.1449. Photograph © 1996, The Art Institute of Chicago.

Medical Equipment

Fill in an early pit in the southeast fort bastion contained a surgeon's tool. It is a *spatula mundani*, so named by 17th-century surgeon John Woodall, who takes credit for devising it and who illustrates it in his 1617 edition of *The Surgion s Mate*. In 1613 the East India Company employed Woodall as its surgeon general. Among his many duties, he was specifically charged with equipping the surgeons' chests for sea voyages. The repetitive nature of this duty led Woodall, "being wearied with writing for every Shippe the same instructions a new," to write his textbook on medicines, treatments, and instruments. Prior to 1613, Woodall resided in London where he was largely engaged in treating plague victims. It was during this time that Woodall apparently sent an equipped surgeon's chest, probably containing a *spatula mundani*, to the Jamestown colony by way of his servant George Liste. This gift is recorded in a list of instructions to Sir Thomas Gates from the Virginia Council in May 1609:

> *There beinge one George Liste servant to John woodall and sent ouer by him with a Chest of Cheurgery sufficiently furnished we require you to giue yor licence to willm wilson his fellowe yf the said George Liste doe stay with you to come backe in this passage the better to enfourme vs what medicines and drugges are fittest to be pvided for the vse of the colonie against ye next supply.* [60]

The dual-purpose iron tool is just over 12" long and consists of a spatula on one end. The opposite end is a split and widened "spoon" with a rounded terminal knob. The term *mundani* comes from the word "mundify or mundifie" which is identified in a 1604 dictionary as meaning "to make clean."[61] The tool's purpose is "to serve upon any occasion of extreame costiveness [constipation]...so that no purging medicine neither upward nor downeward administered or taken will work."[62] The "spoon" end of this instrument was to be used to withdraw the "hard excrements" whereas the spatula was probably for stirring preparations and for applying ointments and plasters.

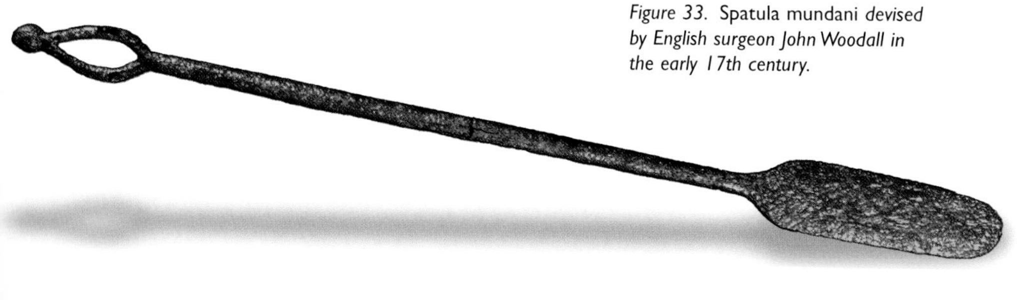

Figure 33. Spatula mundani *devised by English surgeon John Woodall in the early 17th century.*

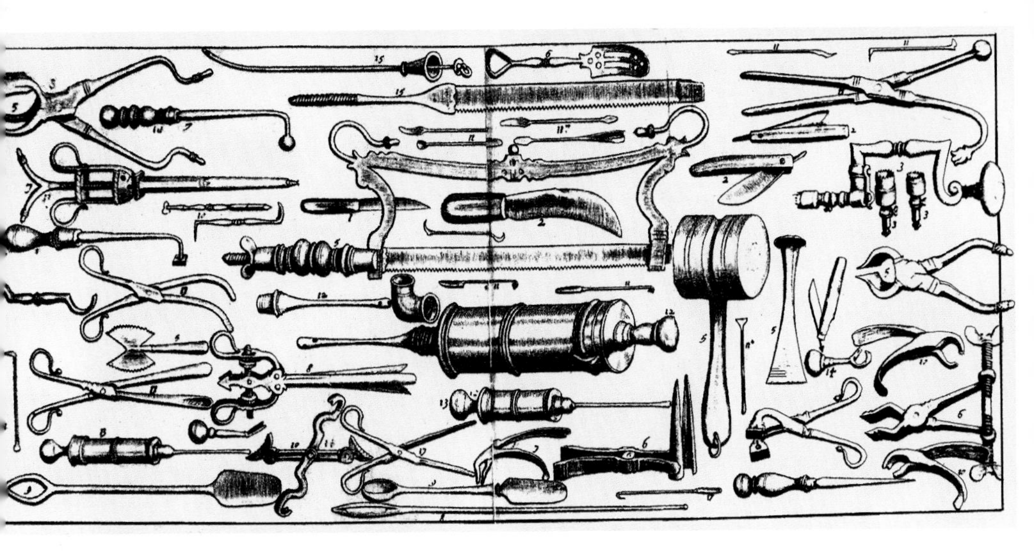

Figure 34. Illustration of tools for the surgeon's chest, taken from John Woodall's The Surgions Mate *published in 1617. The spatula mundani is depicted on the lower left.*

Woodall suggests that fecal impaction is a result of scurvy, although modern medical knowledge does not attribute significant constipation to a deficiency of Vitamin C. It is probably much more likely that this condition was caused by a diet low in fresh fruits and vegetables and by taking large amounts of the opiate laudanum,[63] one of the only effective painkillers known at the time. Woodall extols the virtues of laudanum for "even when through extreamities of paine, the parties are at Deathes doore, or almost madde with the vehemencie of the same, this precious medicine giveth ease presently."[64] Laudanum is particularly prescribed for the "cure of that lamentable disease called Dissenterie, or the bloudy fluxe." Dysentery, along with typhoid and salt poisoning, are believed to have been the primary causes of death in the first few years of the colony.[65]

Coins And Coin Weights

Usually coins are rare finds on archaeological sites, but not so at Jamestown. They are especially welcome discoveries for they are among the few artifacts that bear specific dates and, in turn, establish firm dates for the things with which they are buried whether they be other artifacts or parts of the fort. But they also reveal more than dates.

Sixteen coins and four coin weights have been excavated from the site thus far. This is a very high number for such a relatively small excavated area and indicates the colonists' need for currency, even in what was essentially a barter economy. Only eight of the coins are English, the other eight are Anglo-Irish or Continental coins.

Figure 35. Silver English coins which have been clipped to create small change. Top: Shilling dated by mint mark to 1560-61. Bottom: Half groat dated by mint mark to 1590-92.

Figure 36. Silver English coins fashioned into ornaments, probably for Indian trade. Top: Sixpence cut into a rectangular pendant framing the date 1602. Bottom: Halfgroat of Elizabeth I, minted between 1583 and 1603, which has been rolled into a bead.

Six of the English coins are silver and are from the reign of Elizabeth I, ranging in date from 1560 to 1603. These coins include a shilling, two sixpences, two halfgroats, and one threehalfpence. Three of the coins have been clipped to divide them into change of lesser value. This was a necessary and common practice in England because there was a chronic shortage of money in low denominations which encumbered small monetary transactions. Clipping pieces off of coins was an easy way to make change because, unlike today, the intrinsic value of the metal was equal to the worth of the coin. A halfgroat, worth 2 pence, has been halved into a penny piece, a threehalfpence has been halved to make a coin worth ¾ of a penny, and a shilling, normally worth 12 pence, has been cut into a wedge worth only about 1 ½ pence.

Two of the silver coins have been modified to wear as ornaments, perhaps representing items intended for trade with the Indians. One sixpence has been cut into a rectangular pendant and pierced so as not to obscure the date 1602. A halfgroat has been rolled into a bead in a similar fashion to the copper beads that the colonists were making for trade and that have been recovered from the site. Removed from the conventional market place, these coins are now more valuable to the colonists as jewelry for barter than as legal tender.

Two copper English farthings have also been unearthed from the site. The only discernible markings on one are *REX*, for James I or Charles I, and a crowned harp. It is possibly a Harrington farthing dating ca.1613-1636. In 1636, a rose replaced the crowned harp on the farthing, becoming known as the rose farthing. The second farthing uncovered at the site is one of these rose farthings. It shows little wear and probably was not in circulation long before it was lost.

English coins were made in only gold or silver until 1613, when James I granted a patent to Lord Harrington to produce copper royal farthings. The patent passed to the Duke of Lennox, and the coins continued to be made in the reign of Charles I under the control of the Duchess of Richmond and then Lord Maltravers. These coins "brought enormous profits to the patent holders, but proved not to be popular with the general public"[66] and were discontinued by Parliament in 1644.

The six Anglo-Irish coins consist of five copper pennies and one copper halfpenny minted in England between 1601 and 1602. These coins were made for use in Ireland and did not have wide circulation in England. They would have had little value since silver pennies and halfpennies were in circulation. Ireland had need of these small copper coins, which exchanged at a significant premium because "small silver denominations had been absent from the Irish currency since early in Henry VII's reign."[67]

Figure 37. Irish copper pennies and halfpenny (bottom center) excavated from within James Fort.

It has been suggested that these Irish coins found their way to Virginia in the pockets of individuals who had either seen military service in Ireland or had been involved with the English settlement of Ireland in the early 17th century. It is much more likely that these pennies and halfpennies helped satisfy the need for small change. Just as with Ireland, it was cheaper and more convenient for the English crown to provide the new colony with low denominations in copper rather than silver. The pieces passed as token coinage until silver coinage with intrinsic value was available. Or the answer to their presence may lie with the Indians' penchant for copper. These practically worthless copper coins would make valuable items to trade with the Powhatan.

Two silver coins from the Continent have also been excavated from the site. This is not unusual because the need for small change, already mentioned, led to the widespread use of coinage from the Continent. These coins are also representative of the cosmopolitan nature of trade and travel in the early 17th century.

The Continental coins include a German sechsling and a Dutch two stuiver piece. The sechsling, which is dated 1629, was issued in Lubeck, Germany. Lubeck was part of the Hanseatic League which was a union of towns involved in the east-west trade of the Baltic Sea. The Hanseatic League was formed for the promotion and protection of commerce and by the 15th century dominated European trade. Lubeck merchants were very active in trade all over the world and were particularly involved in the slave trade with the New World.[68]

The Dutch stuiver was minted in Zeeland, in the northern Netherlands, and dates to the second decade of the 17th century. It bears the date 161? with the last number obliterated. These coins were issued as emergency coinage by the seven northern Dutch provinces during their Eighty Years' War with Spain.

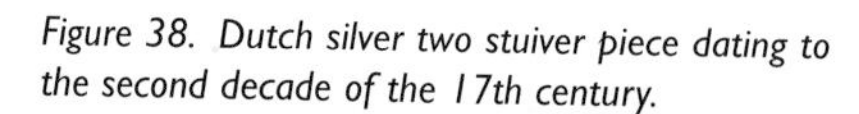

Figure 38. Dutch silver two stuiver piece dating to the second decade of the 17th century.

No gold coins have been excavated from the site but, based on the presence of four coin weights for English gold coins, they were part of the currency at Jamestown. Weights were necessary to verify the values of coins. Since the value of a coin depended upon the intrinsic worth of its gold, silver, or copper, it was a common practice to clip

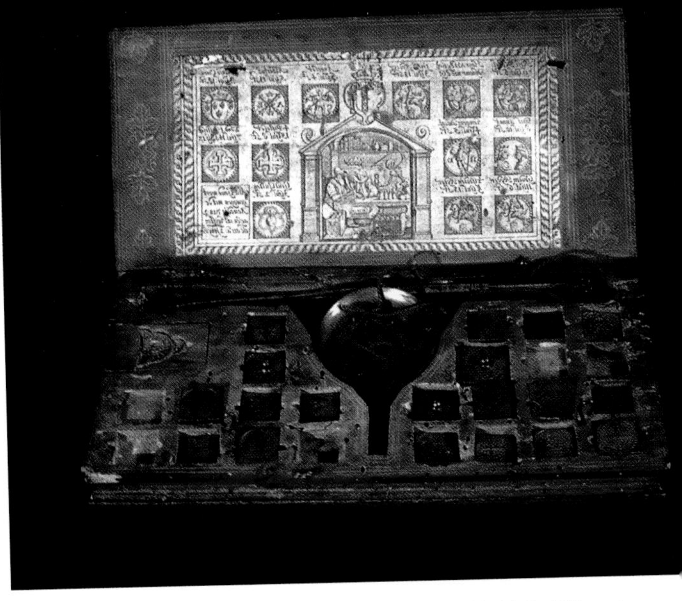

Figure 39. Early 17th-century weight and scale box (above) from Amsterdam.

Figure 40. Brass weights for English gold coins (below). Clockwise from top left: Weight for the gold ryal which was struck during Elizabeth I's reign between 1583 and 1592 and valued at 15 shillings. The hand mark on the reverse signifies that the weight was struck in Antwerp. Top right: Weight for the gold angel depicting St. Michael slaying a dragon. The angel was valued at 11 shillings from 1612-1619. Bottom right: Weight for the gold unite (22 shillings) illustrating the half-length torso of James I with orb and scepter. Bottom left: Weight with the bust of James I for the gold double crown worth 11 shillings.

the coins for the metal. This illegal practice was not always detectable on the hammered coins made before 1662 which, unlike the later machine-made coinage, were not finished with a milled edge.

Coin weights portray the obverse, or front side, of the coin they represent. This was done to enable easy identification and was especially necessary for the largely illiterate population of the time.

All of the weights recovered from the site are square and, although round weights were introduced during the reign of James I, three are for Stuart coins. The only Elizabethan weight is for the gold ryal worth 15 shillings. It is stamped with a hand, indicating that it was made in Antwerp, and bears the maker's initials "PVG." The Elizabethan ryal was issued between 1583 and 1592.

The three Stuart weights all date between 1612 and 1619 and may have formed part of the same set. Coin weights were sold in portable boxed sets complete with scales. The weights are for an angel, worth 11 shillings; a unite, valued at 22 shillings; and a double crown of 11 shillings. They each bear a deeply stamped secondary impression of a crowned *I*, for King James, which may be the mark of the government official validating each weight's accuracy. This practice started with a 1491 statue of Henry VII, causing all standard brass weights and measures to be stamped with a crowned *H*. Weights bearing the crowned *C* from Charles I's reign (1625-1649) are also known.

A "King's Touch" Token?

Two coin-like copper objects were recovered from the site that may relate to an English practice that originated in the 14th century and that imbues the monarch with godlike powers of healing. The objects, which are stamped only on one side with an intertwined rose and thistle under a crown, have been identified as "King's Touch" tokens.[69] The touch of the King (or Queen) was believed to cure the "King's Evil" or scrofula, a disease of the lymph glands. The king would lay his hand upon the diseased area and bless the afflicted in a ritual set down in the *Book of Common Prayer*. The diseased person would then be given a "touch-piece" as a token of the ceremony.

The rose and thistle identifies the token with James I, who used this motif on the halfgroat, penny, and halfpenny to acknowledge the union of England and Scotland.[70] Three other King's Touch tokens have been

Figure 41. Illuminated manuscript (above) from the Mary Tudor Prayer Book illustrating Queen Mary touching for the "King's Evil." All Tudor and Stuart monarchs participated in this healing ceremony.

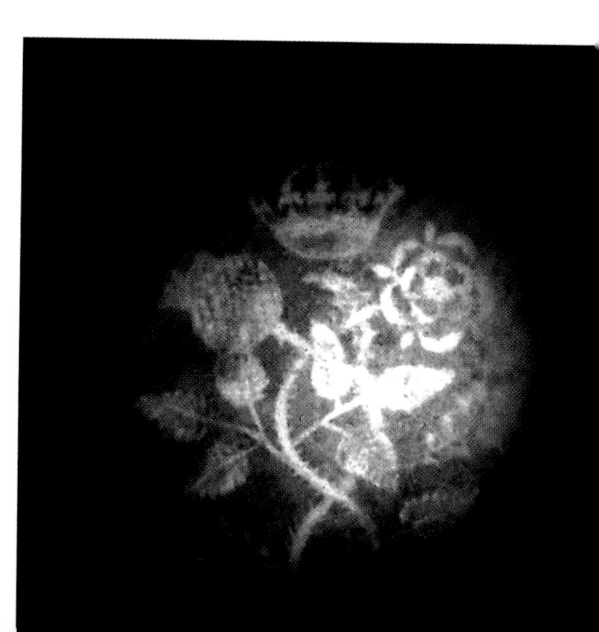

Figure 42. X ray of the King's Touch token (right) excavated from Ditch I within James Fort.

found in the Jamestown area in contexts of the 1620s and 30s.[71] Although all the Stuart rulers exercised the gift of touching, these tokens most likely do not represent a ceremony for the King's Evil in Virginia. Like the Irish coinage, they probably represent inexpensive copper items for the Indian trade.

A Complete Jug

In the fall of 1996 a complete vessel was uncovered during excavations in the bulwark ditch. This remarkable find is an early 17th-century Border ware drinking jug. The Border ware potteries were located in the border area (hence the name) of Hampshire and Surrey counties in England. They were the chief suppliers of earthenwares to London during the 16th and 17th centuries.[72]

Complete ceramic vessels are rare finds on archaeological sites of colonial Virginia. This is because most of these predominantly earthenware and stoneware objects were used on a daily basis to store, prepare, and consume food and beverages. Regular use subjected these artifacts to a far greater chance of breaking than vessels that were meant solely for display or were saved for ceremonial purposes. This is important for archaeologists because ceramic objects tend to break and be discarded within a short time after purchase. Ceramic history has been well researched and much is known about the dates of production and the forms and decoration of the various wares available during the colonial period. This knowledge of date and function makes ceramics one of the most valuable classes of artifact for the archaeologist to use in interpreting a site.

The Jamestown Border ware jug is a very thin, buff earthenware which has been roughly covered over the upper half with olive green lead glaze. Despite the pouring spout located opposite to the handle, documentary evidence suggests this form to be a drinking vessel for a single serving of wine or beer.[73] The liquid would literally be poured down the throat! Many of these drinking jugs were excavated from the site of the Inns of Court in London. This institution, where students read the law, maintained detailed accounts in which "beer pottes" from the Border ware potteries were frequently mentioned. These vessels had to be replaced frequently as a result of breakage–sometimes from the students expressing displeasure with their professors–and theft. The high replacement rate led to the request in 1615 that

> *every Bencher and Utter Barrister's Clerk shall provide a pot about the size and quantity of the green pots now used in the House at their own charges, and that they*

shall not carry away any of the green pots.[74]

While it cannot be said for sure that the Border ware drinking jug found in the bulwark ditch was a container for beer, as in its traditional usage, it is known that beer was a standard commodity on all English ships at the time. That it was not plentiful in the colony in the early years seems certain, as it is one of the items the sailors on each incoming vessel could exchange with unscrupulous colonists for unauthorized access to Indian "furres, baskets, mussaneekes, young beastes or such like commodities." By the late 1620s, the colonists were brewing their own beer. John Smith records in 1629 that "for drinke, some [Virginia colonists] malt the Indian corne, others barley, of which they make good ale, both strong and small.[75] Foundations of a brewery dating to this time period were uncovered during excavations in the 1950s in the New Towne area of Jamestown.[76]

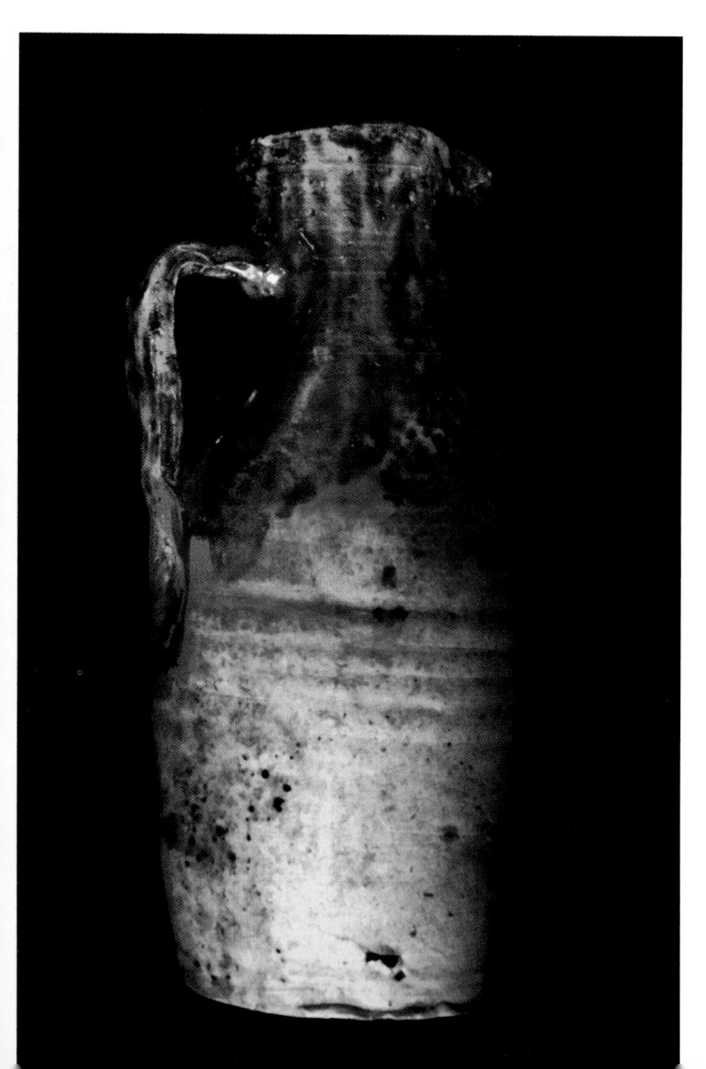

Figure 43. A complete Border ware drinking jug excavated from within the bulwark ditch of James Fort.

Conclusion

Indeed, through the interplay of documents and artifacts, *APVA Jamestown Rediscovery* offers a number of revelations about "James Fort" and early "James Towne". Discovery of the fort site on the most strategic piece of ground on the Island and Dutch tokens of the 16th century combine to pose questions about the extent of military experience among the first Jamestown "gentlemen" and their Dutch connection. Another look at documents established that, well into the 1620s, all of the presidents, governors and a great number of other Jamestown colonists accumulated years of combat experience in the Eighty Years' War in the Netherlands. Knowledge of their military skills is an important fact to consider when trying to determine how well suited they were for the task of settlement. Certainly what they had learned on the Continent served the English well in their invasion of alien Virginia. Apparently the Virginia Company officials chose Virginia recruits wisely. And while the timber "stick" enclosure of James Fort and obsolete arms, armor, and other supplies pale in comparison to European fortresses and state-of-the-art equipment of 1607, they proved to be adequate defense against the actual enemy—the Powhatans. The Virginia Company also had the foresight to supply the colony with up-to-date medical supplies and exactly the right copper stock for the craftsmen to fashion jewelry to trade with Virginia Indians. So it seems, this early attempt to establish a permanent English colony by the businessmen of London was not quite as poorly planned and supported as other evidence often suggests.

In any event, three seasons of excavation have only begun to unlock the secrets of what is now quite possibly a four-acre fort and adjacent living area. It is clear that it will take years of field and analytical research to more fully comprehend the "Fort" and the "Towne's" original plan, as well as the growth and development of the community and the day-to-day lives of its early residents. The observance of English America's 400th anniversary in 2007 is now only ten years away. Based on the amazing preliminary "search" excavations of 1994-96, there is every reason to expect that the future *APVA Jamestown Rediscovery* program will add yet more significant chapters to what is becoming a very full Jamestown story.

WMK

Figure 44. A 1590 copper token issued at Groningen, northern Netherlands, found at Jamestown.

Endnotes

[1] However, John Smith indicates that the 'Dutchmen" among the settlers were teaching the Indians to use firearms. Philip L. Barbour, ed., *The Complete Works of Captain John Smith (1580-1631)* (Chapel Hill: The Univ. of North Carolina Press, 1986), 1:259-260.

[2] George Percy, [1608?] *Observations gathered out of "A Discourse of the Southern Colony in Virginia by the English, 1606,"* ed. by David B. Quinn (Charlottesville, VA: Univ. Press of Virginia, 1967), 24-27.

[3] Ibid.

[4] Barbour, *John Smith*, 1:41.

[5] Alexander Brown, *Genesis of the United States* (Boston: Houghton, Mifflin and Co., 1890), Vol. 2, passim.

[6] William Strachey, "A True Reportory of the Wreck and Redemption of Sir Thomas Gates, Knight," in *A Voyage to Virginia in 1609*, ed. Louis B. Wright (Charlottesville, VA: Univ. Press of Virginia, 1964), 15.

[7] William Shakespeare, *The Tempest*, Act I, Scene 1.

[8] Strachey, "True Reportory," Chapter 1.

[9] S. G. Culliford, *William Strachey, 1572-1621*, (Charlottesville, VA: Univ. Press of Virginia, 1965), 140.

[10] Strachey, "True Reportory," 79.

[11] Percy, *Observations*, 22.

[12] Barbour, *John Smith*, 2:325.

[13] Barbour, *John Smith*, 2:180-181.

[14] Detailed architectural study of the tower remains to be done. Still, according to Geoff Parnell (Royal Armouries, HM Tower of London), regardless of when the tower was built, the loopholes indicate that it could be used for defense as well as a bell tower.

[15] Paul Ive, [1589] *The Practise of Fortification* (New York: Da Capo Press, 1968), Chapter 3.

[16] Clifford M. Lewis and Albert J. Loomie, *The Spanish Jesuit Mission in Virginia, 1570-1572*, (Raleigh: University of North Carolina Press, 1953), passim.

[17] David B. Quinn, *North America From Earliest Discovery to First Settlements* (New York: Harper & Row, 1978), 433-434.

[18] David B. Quinn, *Set Fair for Roanoke* (Raleigh: University of North Carolina Press, 1985), passim.

[19] Percy, *Observations*, 8.

[20] Ibid., 10-11.

[21] Ibid., 8.

[22] Philip L. Barbour, *The Jamestown Voyages Under the First Charter 1606-1609* (Cambridge: The University Press, 1969), 254-260.

[23] Quinn, *North America*, 245-258.

[24] Barbour, *Jamestown Voyages*, 115-121, 254-260.

[25] J. Leitch Wright, *Anglo-Spanish Rivalry in North America*, (Athens: University of Georgia Press, 1971), 35.

[26] Barbour, *John Smith*, 1:41.

[27] Ibid., 266.

[28] Wright, *Anglo-Spanish*, 38-41.

[29] Susan M. Kingsbury, ed., *The Records of the Virginia Company of London* (Washington: Government Printing Office, 1906), 3:243-244.

[30] Fyne Morrison in David Beers Quinn, *The Elizabethans and the Irish*, (Ithaca, NY: Cornell Univ. Press, 1966), 41.

[31] Earl of Sussex in Grenfell Morton, *Elizabethan Ireland* (Harlow: Longman, 1971), 26-27.

[32] Ive, *Practise of Fortification*, epistle dedicatorie.

[33] Richard Norwood, [1639] *Fortification or Architecture Military* (New York: Da Capo Press, 1973), 125.

[34] For a complete treatment of the Roanoke expeditions see David Quinn's *Set Fair for Roanoke*.

[35] David B. Quinn, ed., *The Roanoke Voyages 1584-1590* (New York: Dover Publications, 1991), 1:130-139.

[36] Two major examples of this newly acquired knowledge are Thomas Hariot's 1588 book *A Briefe and True Report on the New Found Land of Virginia* and John White's *Map of Virginia*.

[37] Ive, *Practise of Fortification*, 6-7.

[38] Jean C. Harrington, *Search for the Cittie of Raleifh, Archaeological Excavations at Fort Raleigh National Historic Site, North Carolina*, Archaeological Research Series Number Six (Washington D.C.: National Park Service, U.S. Department of the Interior, 1962), 9-17.

[39] Nicholas M. Luccketti. "Smith's Fort," *Discovery* XV, (1982) no. 2.

[40] Barbour, *Jamestown Voyages*, 1:49-54.

[41] Ibid., 109.

[42] Wright, *Anglo-Spanish*, 63.

[43] Eric Speth, Maritime Services Manager for Jamestown Settlement and Captain of the reconstructed Virginia's First Fleet consisting of the Susan Constant, Godspeed, and Discovery.

[44] Barbour, *John Smith*, 2:263.

[45] Speth, Jamestown Settlement.

[46] Percy, *Observations*, 15-16.

[47] Barbour, *John Smith*, 2:325.

[48] O. F. G. Hogg, *English Artillery 1326-1716* (London: Royal Artillery Institution, 1963), 26.

[49] Other scholars have previously arrived at this conclusion, for example, Edmund B. Morgan in his *American Slavery/American Freedom*; J. Leitch Wright in *Anglo-Spanish Rivalry in North America*; David Hawke in *The Colonial Experience*; and John Reps in *Tidewater Towns*.

[50] Kingsbury, *Records*, 3:676.

[51] Barbour, *John Smith*, 2:189.

[52] George Percy, [1611] "Letter," *Percy Family, Letters and Papers*, IX (1608-1617), f.173, as quoted in John W. Shirley "George Percy at Jamestown, 1607-1612," *The Virginia Magazine of History and Biography* 57 no. 3 (1949): 239.

[53] Kingsbury, *Records*, 3:456.

[54] Barbour, *John Smith*, 1:35.

[55] Patrick M. Malone, *The Skulking Way of War: Technology and Tactics Among the New England Indians*, (New York: London, 1990), 17.

[56] Randle Holme [1688] *The Academy of Armory* (Ann Arbor, Michigan: Xerox University Microfilms, 1975), 2:5.

[57] Kingsbury, *Records*, 3:665.

[58] Barbour, *John Smith*, 2:146.

[59] Henry Porter, [1599] *The Two Angrie Women of Abington* quoted in A.V.B. Norman *The Rapier and the Small-Sword, 1460-1820* (New York: Arno Press, 1980), 25.

[60] Kingsbury, *Records*, 3:23. The servant with the chest may have arrived in Virginia before Gates and his instructions. Gates sailed aboard the *Sea Venture*, which was borne off course by storms and wrecked on Bermuda. Seven of the eight other ships comprising the fleet that sailed with the *Sea Venture* arrived in Virginia in August 1609. Gates did not reach Virginia until the following year.

[61] Robert Caudrey [1604] *A Table Alphabeticall of Hard Unusual English Words*. Robert A. Peters, ed. (Gainesville, FL: Scholars' Facsimiles & Reprints, 1966).

[62] John Woodall, *The Surgions Mate* (1617; reprint with foreword by John Kirkup, Bath: Kingsmead, 1978), 14.

[63] Dennis A.J. Morey, M.D., personal communication, 1977.

[64] Woodall, *Surgions Mate*, 225.

[65] Carville V. Earle, "Environment, Disease, and Mortality in Early Virginia," *The Chesapeake in the Seventeenth Century*, ed. Thad W. Tate and David L. Ammerman (Raleigh: The Univ. of North Carolina Press, 1979), 96-125.

[66] J.J. North, *English Hammered Coinage Volume 2*, (London: Spink & Son, 1991), 20.

[67] John Stafford-Langan, personal communication, 1997.

[68] D. Antjekathrin Grassmann, personal communication, 1995.

[69] Alice L.L. Ferguson and T.D. Stewart, "An Ossuary near Piscataway Creek with a Report on the Skeletal Remains," *American Antiquity* 6 (1940): 13.

[70] North, *Hammered Coinage*, 20, 150.

[71] One was found during National Park Service excavations at Jamestown; one was located at The Maine (ca. 1618-1625) near Jamestown, and one was excavated at Flowerdew Hundred, about 25 river miles from Jamestown. Eighteen of the tokens, pierced and comprising a necklace, were located in a 17th-century Indian ossuary on the banks of Piscataway Creek in Maryland (Ferguson and Stewart, *Ossuary*).

[72] Jacqueline Pearce, *Border Wares*, (London: HMSO, 1992), 102.

[73] L.G. Matthews and H. J. M. Green, "Post-Medieval Pottery of the Inns of Court," *Post-Medieval Archaeology* 3 (1969): 1-17.

[74] C.T. Martin, ed., (1904) *Middle Temple Records*, 2:596, as quoted in Matthews and Green, "Post-Medieval Pottery," 3.

[75] Barbour, *John Smith*, 3:216.

[76] John L. Cotter, *Archeological Excavations at Jamestown, Virginia*, reprint of 1958 edition (Washington, D.C.: U.S. Department of the Interior, 1994), 102-109.

Illustration Credits

Figure 3: *Portrait of George Percy #854.2*, courtesy of Virginia Historical Society, Richmond, VA.

Figure 4: Courtesy National Park Service, Colonial National Historical Park.

Figure 5: Courtesy National Park Service, Colonial National Historical Park.

Figure 6: Courtesy of Office of the Governor, Richmond, VA.

Figure 7: Top, "First Folio Shakespeare Engraving," courtesy of the Folger Shakespeare Library. Bottom, *Sea Venture* by Deryck Foster, reprinted by kind courtesy of the Bank of Bermuda.

Figure 9: "Jamestown 1619 by Sidney King," courtesy of National Park Service, Colonial National Historical Park.

Figure 12: *Site of Jamestown*, 19th-century lithograph by F. B. Shell, engraved by H. S. Beckwith, transferred to glass and painted by John S. Carow, APVA.

Figure 17: *The Little Fortress on the Bank of the River* by Robert van den Hoeke.

Figure 22: Reproduced by permission of Edinburgh University Library from John Derrick's *The Image of Ireland*, 1581 (De.3.76).

Figure 23: *Leiden* from Georg Braun and Frans Hogenberg, *Civitates orbis terrarum.*

Figure 24: *Map of Raleigh's Virginia* by John White, ca. 1585. Copyright British Museum.

Figure 25: *Building of Charlesfort in Santa Elena* by T. de Bry, *America*, II, 1591, pl. 10, after drawing by Jacques de Moyne. Courtesy of Special Collections Department, University of Virginia Library.

Figure 26: *Building of Fort Caroline on St. John's River* by T. de Bry, *America*, II, 1591, pl. 10, after a drawing by Jacques de Moyne. Courtesy of Special Collections Department, University of Virginia Library.

Figure 27: *Manuscript plan of Armagh and the Fort at Blackwater Northern Ireland,* Richard Barlett. Courtesy of the National Library of Ireland.

Figure 29: Algemeen Rijksarchief, Den Haag, Netherlands.

Figure 31: Top: (JR105D) diameter: 14.8 cm. Middle: Detail from *A Fete at Bermondsey,* ca. 1570, by J Hoefnagel. Reproduction is by courtesy of the Marquess of Salisbury; photo by The Fotomas Index. Bottom: Detail from *Embarkation of Henry VIII*, Unknown, The Royal Collection © Her Majesty the Queen Elizabeth II. Quote from Edward Howes, [1615] *The annales of the antiquarian John Stow augmented into the ende of this present yeere 1614*, in A.V.B. Norman, *Rapier and Small Sword 1460-1820* (London: Arms and Armour Press, 1990),p. 869.

Figure 32: Top: (446-JR) length: 41 cm, width: 35 cm. Middle: Courtesy Virginia Department of Historic Resources. Bottom: Albrecht Dürer, German, 1471-1528, *The Knight, Death and the Devil*, engraving, 1513, 24.4 x 18.8 cm, Clarence Buckingham Collection, (1938.1449). Photograph © 1996, The Art Institute of Chicago. All rights reserved.

Figure 33: (447-JR) length 32 cm.

Figure 34: *Instruments for East India Co. Chest*, from *The Surgions Mate*, by John Woodall, 1617. Bristol University Medical School.

Figure 35: Top: (41-JR) length 10 mm, width 10 mm. Bottom: (38-JR) diameter 17mm.

Figure 36: Top: (89-JR) length 12 mm, width 10 mm. Bottom: (728-JR) length 15 mm, width 5mm.

Figure 37: (42-JR, 92-JR, 101-JR, 724-JR, 725-JR) penny diameters range from 14-18 mm; (726-JR) halfpenny diameter: 13 mm.

Figure 38: (144-JR) diameter: 20 mm.

Figure 39: Courtesy of Hunter and Margolin Antiques, Yorktown, VA.

Figure 40: Top left: (91-JR) width 13 mm. Top right: (16-JR) width 11 mm. Bottom right: (421-JR) width 14mm. Bottom left: (37-JR) width 11 mm.

Figure 41: *Queen Mary Touching for the King's Evil.* Reproduced with the permission of the Reverend Monsignor George Stack, Administrator of Westminster Cathedral, London.

Figure 43: (688-JR) height of jug, 190mm.

Figure 44: (424-JR) diameter 23mm.

Back Cover: Photos courtesy of Ira Block, Kenneth Lyons, and David Hazzard.